KT-419-713

INTRODU

Eastern Philosophy

Richard Osborne and Borin Van Loon

Edited by Richard Appignanesi

ICON BOOKS UK

TOTEM BOOKS USA

This edition published in the UK
in 2000 by Icon Books Ltd.,
Grange Road, Duxford,
Cambridge CB2 4QF
E-mail: info@iconbooks.co.uk
www.iconbooks.co.uk

Sold in the UK, Europe, South Africa
and Asia by Faber and Faber Ltd.,
3 Queen Square, London WC1N 3AU
or their agents

Distributed in the UK, Europe,
South Africa and Asia by
Macmillan Distribution Ltd.,
Houndmills, Basingstoke RG21 6XS

This edition published in Australia
in 2000 by Allen & Unwin Pty. Ltd.,
PO Box 8500, 83 Alexander Street,
Crows Nest, NSW 2065

Previously published in the UK and
Australia in 1996 under the title
Ancient Eastern Philosophy for Beginners

Reprinted 1998, 2000, 2001

First published in the United States
in 1996 by Totem Books
Inquiries to: Icon Books Ltd.,
Grange Road, Duxford,
Cambridge CB2 4QF, UK
email: info@iconbooks.co.uk
www.iconbooks.co.uk

In the United States,
distributed to the trade by
National Book Network Inc.,
4720 Boston Way, Lanham,
Maryland 20706

Distributed in Canada by
Penguin Books Canada,
10 Alcorn Avenue, Suite 300,
Toronto, Ontario M4V 3B2

ISBN 1 84046 150 0

Text copyright © 1996 Richard Osborne
Illustrations copyright © 1996 Borin Van Loon

The author and artist have asserted their moral rights.

Originating editor: Richard Appignanesi

No part of this book may be reproduced in any form, or by any means,
without prior permission in writing from the publisher.

Printed and bound in Australia
by McPherson's Printing Group, Victoria

What is Eastern philosophy? How is it different to Western philosophy? Can Westerners understand Eastern philosophy, given the huge cultural and language difference between the East and the West? These are some of the very tricky questions we will be getting at in this guide to beginning Eastern philosophy.

Philosophy, we might say, is the search for knowledge and for a means to express it, and Eastern philosophy has many forms of both.

So, What is Eastern Philosophy?

One answer would be that it is a vast collection of philosophical and religious ideas that derive from the ancient cultures of India, China, Persia, Japan, Korea, Egypt, Tibet, etc, and from many different traditions and forms of thought that shaped the development of the East from earliest recorded times.

Eastern philosophy is a multi-faceted set of ideas that deeply reflect the complex societies they grew out of.

So, all you need to know is the complex history of the Eastern world, how to speak several languages, read forty thousand volumes of Sanskrit and Chinese, meditate and sit in one position for nine years without moving.
Who knows his own nature knows heaven. So what is our true self? That is the central question.
—Sankara
But you have to start somewhere . . . and in one sense, Eastern philosophy is exactly the same as Western philosophy in that it tries to explain the world we live in and what shapes it. It just comes up with different answers!

Beginning Somewhere . . .

But the question still remains of beginning **somewhere** in Eastern philosophy, of limiting the area to manageable proportions for the beginner. Here is a map that shows some of the origins of Eastern thought and also just how extensive, both in space and time, the subject is.

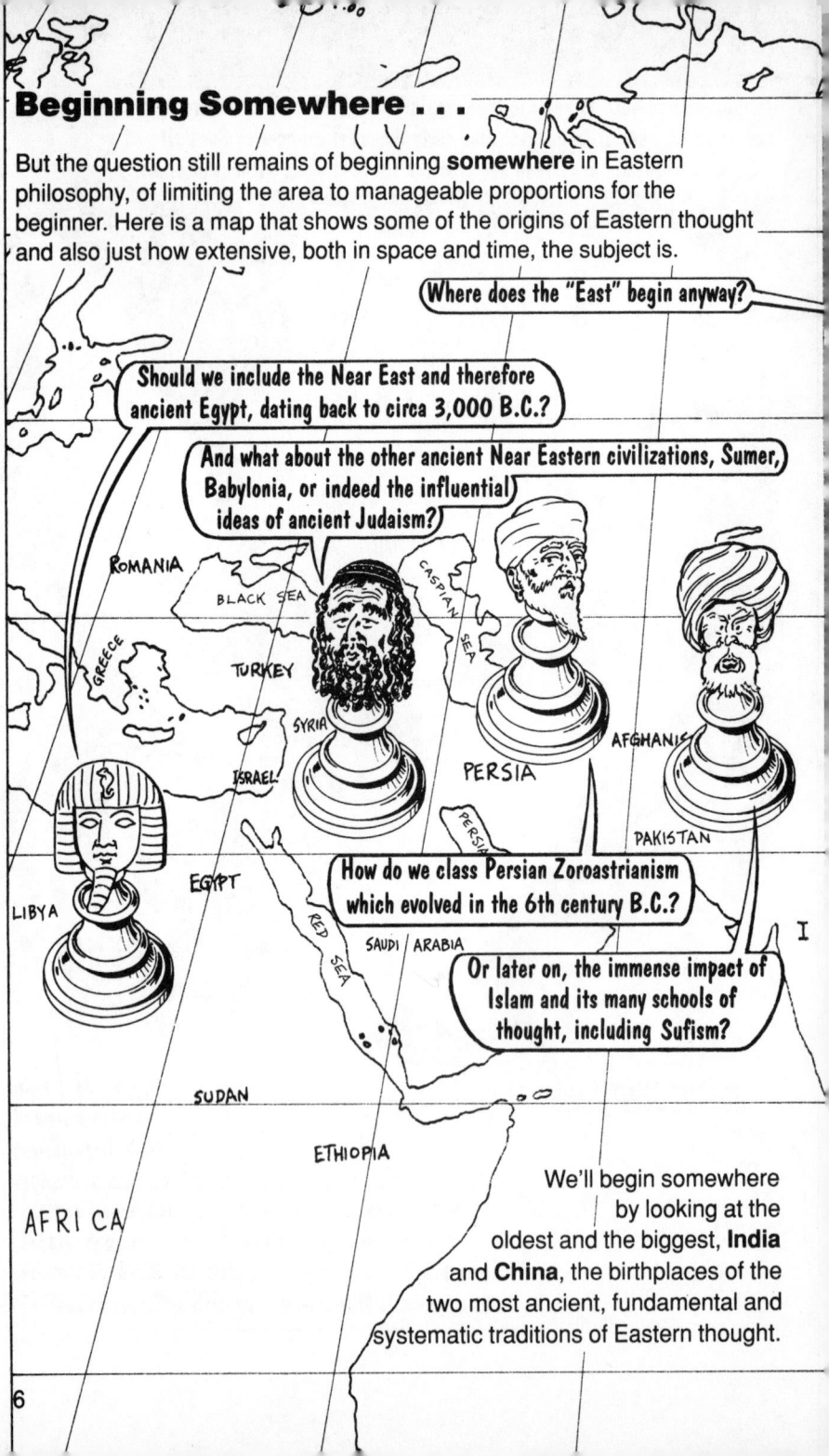

We'll begin somewhere by looking at the oldest and the biggest, **India** and **China**, the birthplaces of the two most ancient, fundamental and systematic traditions of Eastern thought.

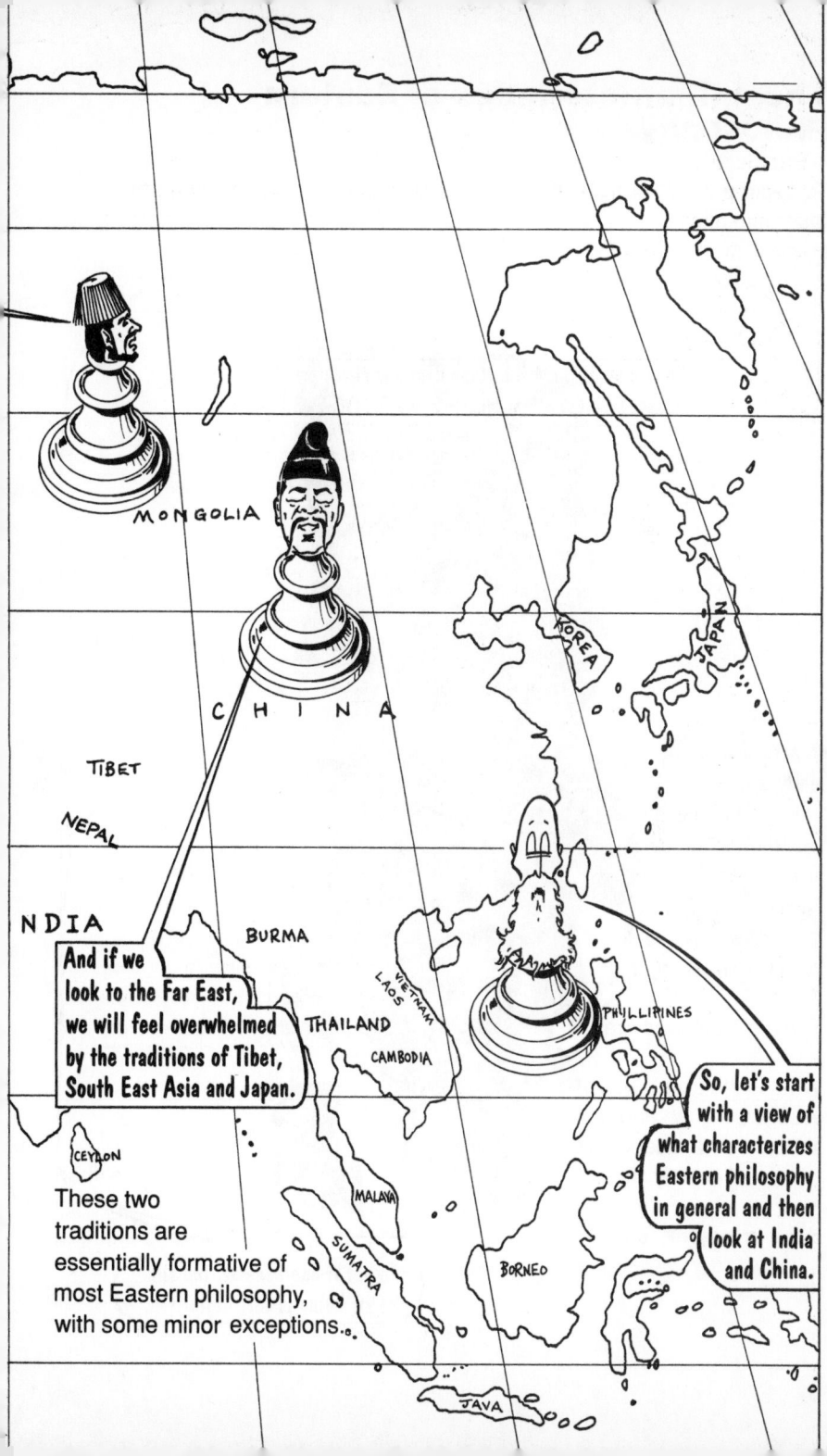
MONGOLIA
CHINA
TIBET
NEPAL
NDIA
BURMA
THAILAND
LAOS
VIETNAM
CAMBODIA
KOREA
JAPAN
PHILLIPINES
CEYLON
MALAYA
SUMATRA
BORNEO
JAVA
And if we look to the Far East, we will feel overwhelmed by the traditions of Tibet, South East Asia and Japan.
So, let's start with a view of what characterizes Eastern philosophy in general and then look at India and China.
These two traditions are essentially formative of most Eastern philosophy, with some minor exceptions.

The 4 Characteristics of Eastern Philosophy

To begin with, we can say that Eastern philosophy is characterized by four main aims.

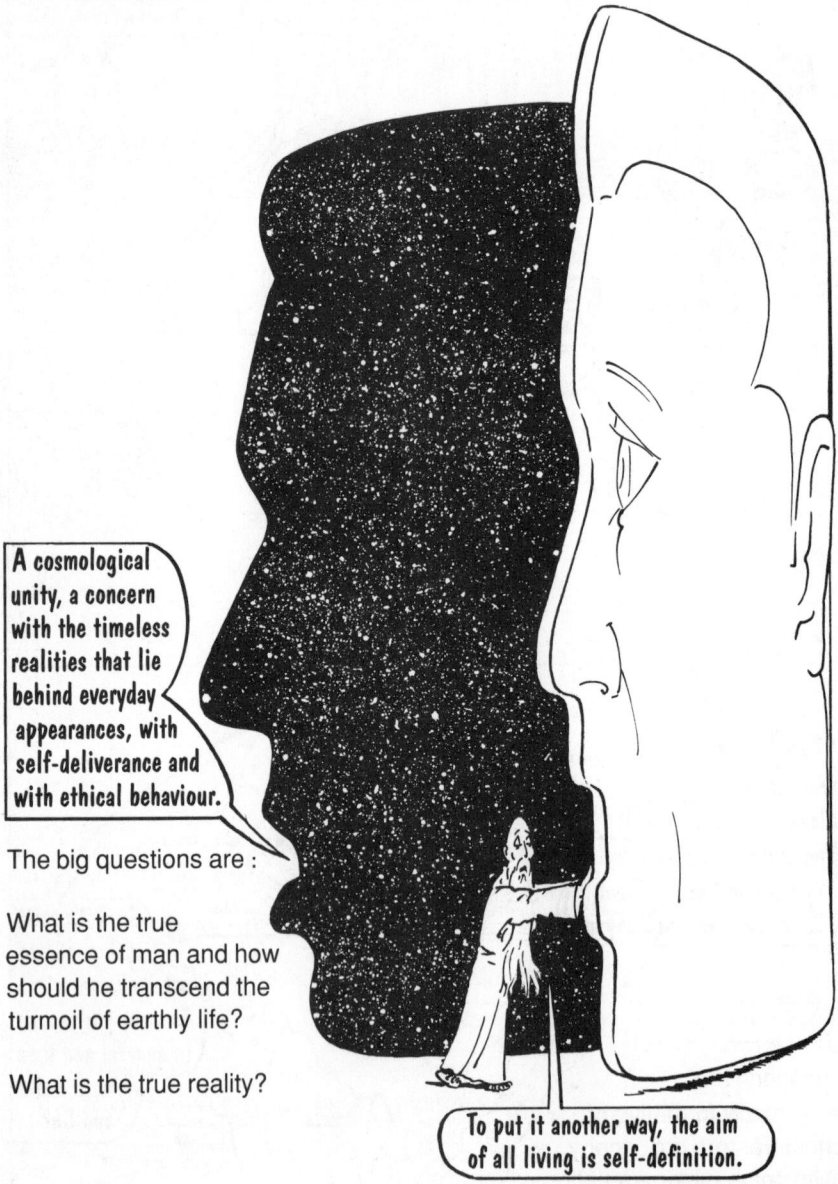

The big questions are :

What is the true essence of man and how should he transcend the turmoil of earthly life?

What is the true reality?

To sum up, the three main strands are Chinese, Indian and Japanese, and there are major differences as well as similarities.

Eastern philosophy has been concerned with suffering, the self, the sublime and the nature of everlasting being.
Man is part of the never-ending cycle of being and death (Hindus call it **Samsara**). No one can escape that reality. But man also lives in society and must contend with that. There are many differences in expressing the way of Enlightenment and the nature of being. Eastern philosophy has a very different notion of the self to Western philosophy, one that accepts the never-ending reality of an all-existing truth.
Is that the idea that liberation comes from getting away from the false self and finding the true self?
That is one of the approaches within Eastern philosophy. There are many paths, but only one road!

East or West . . . Which is Best?

Eastern and Western traditions in philosophy have often intersected throughout the ages. In fact, the survival of ancient Greek philosophy owed much to Arab scholars during the Middle Ages.

Unfortunately, we tend to divide the world up into these two great traditions, Eastern and Western, and we all like to think in opposites, good/bad, black/white, right/wrong, etc.

That we are perhaps reaching a stage where these oppositions may be overcome is indicative either of a spiritual re-awakening or a truly global market, or both.

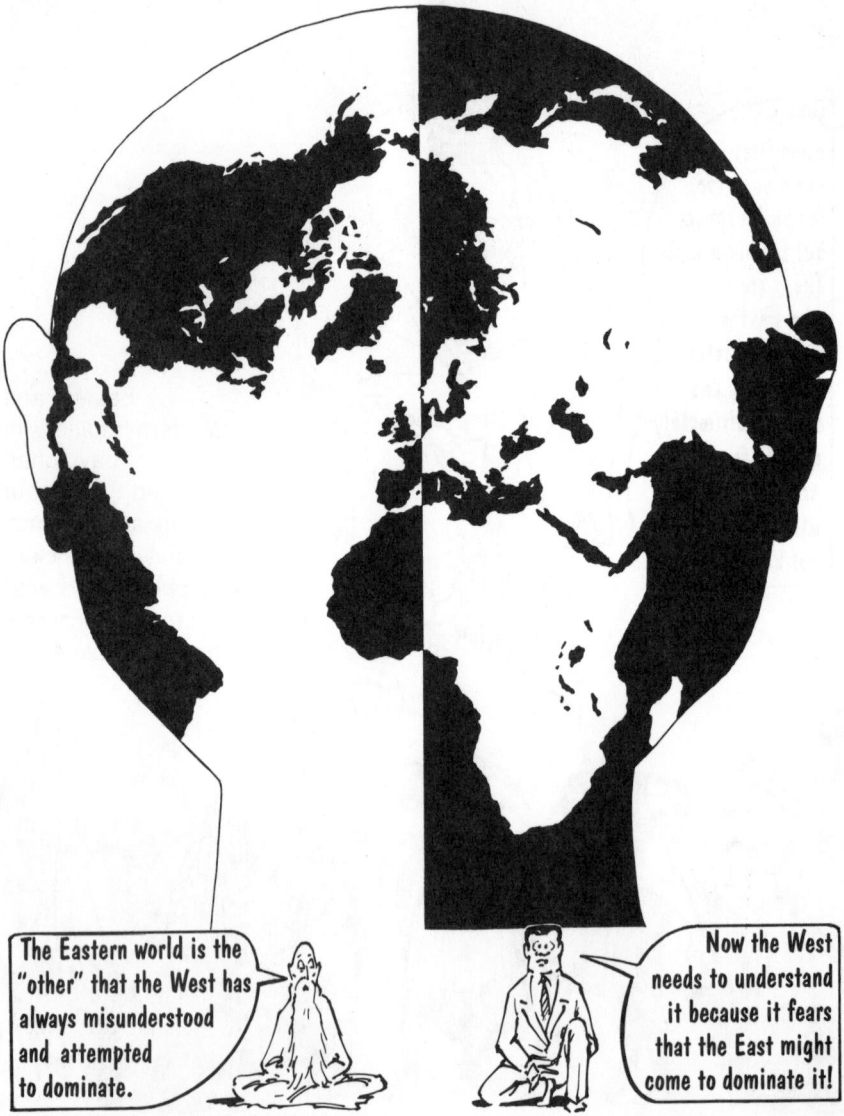

Is Eastern Philosophy just Religion?

Perhaps the one major distinction between Eastern and Western philosophy is that the Eastern tradition does not attempt to distinguish clearly between philosophy and religion. This, of course, leads to some problems. For example, Buddhism as a philosophy is often confused with the religious practices that grew out of it.

Eastern Philosophy v. Western Philosophy?

Since the two traditions are always thought of in opposition to each other, it is perhaps worth looking again at some of the similarities and differences.

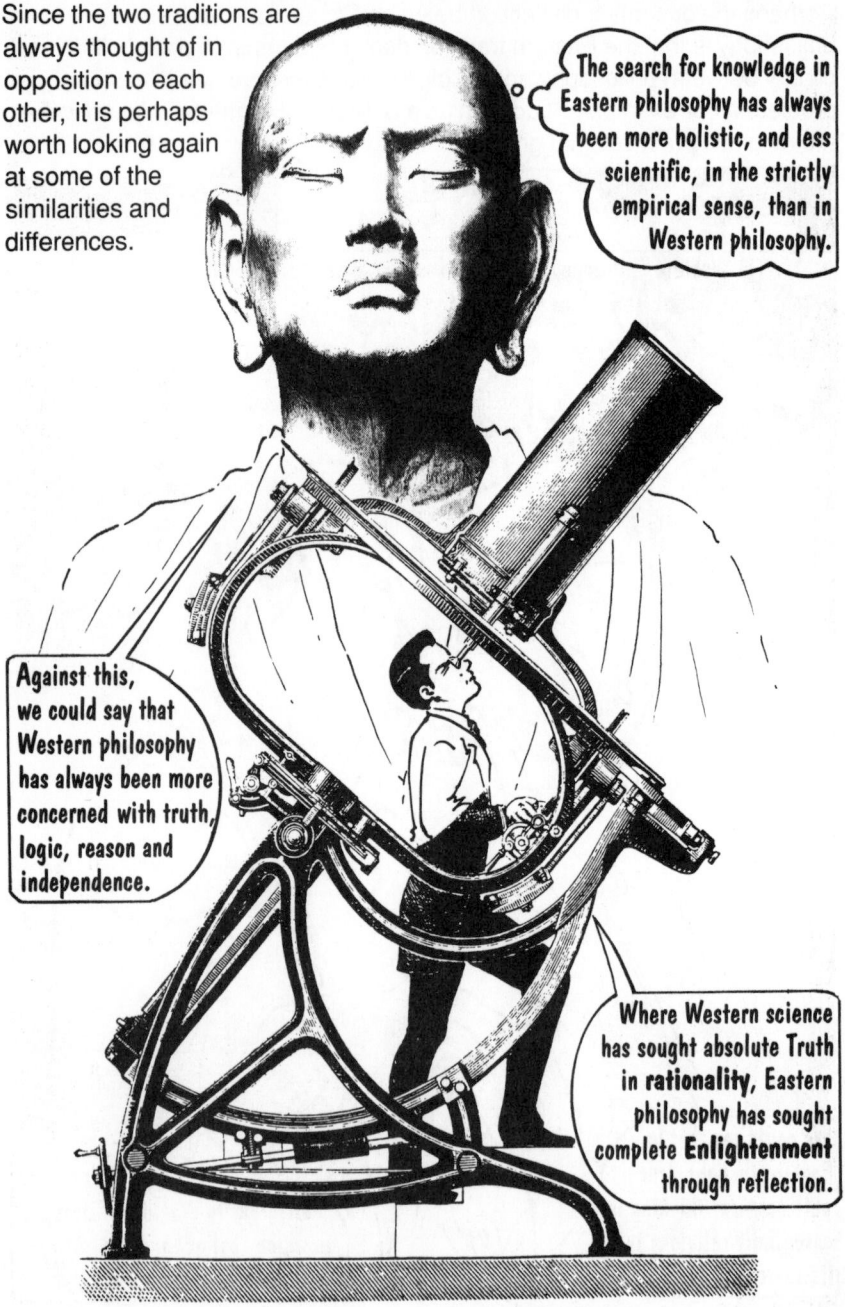

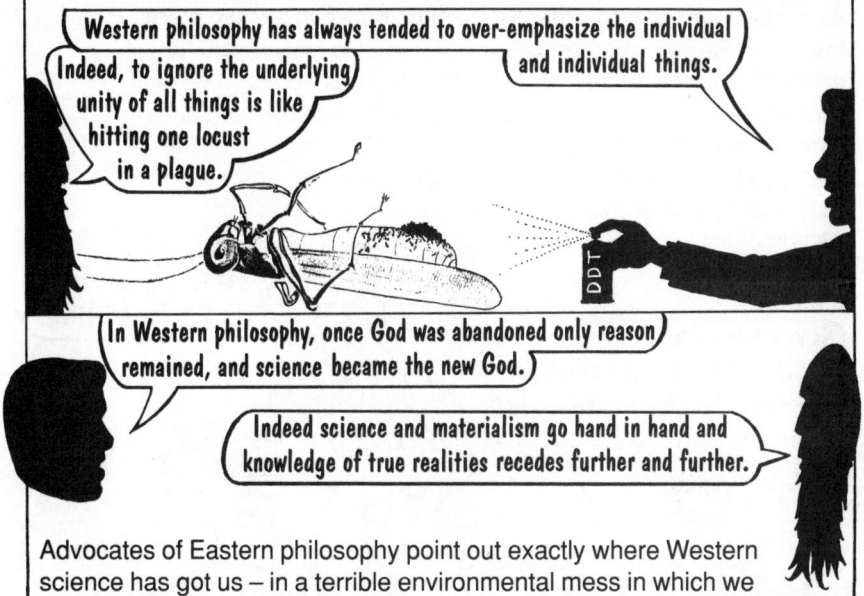

Advocates of Eastern philosophy point out exactly where Western science has got us – in a terrible environmental mess in which we need the insights of Eastern philosophy to bring us back into harmony with the earth and the cosmos.

As a general description of the difference between the two great traditions, we can say that the Eastern tends to look inward for the essential answers about man whilst the Western looks outward to the absolute and to the social and political. At the same time, Eastern thought resolutely believes in the interconnectedness of all things and of the need to escape from the limits of individualism, which is connected with bodily pleasures and the illusion of separateness.

What is Real?

Hegel, a great Western philosopher, said . . .

Hegel probably means that only those things that can be coherently, sensibly argued for can be proven and taken as the real. The Tao probably means that the true nature of ultimate reality is almost unknowable and probably impossible to communicate. (Oddly enough, there are influences of Eastern philosophy in Hegel, but that is another story.)

In contrast to the Western idealization of power, money and science, Eastern traditions have honoured the thinker, the sage, the poet and the mystic. Eastern traditions declare the reality of the unseen world and venerate the call of spiritual life. This is a very fundamental difference.

India: Language Distribution

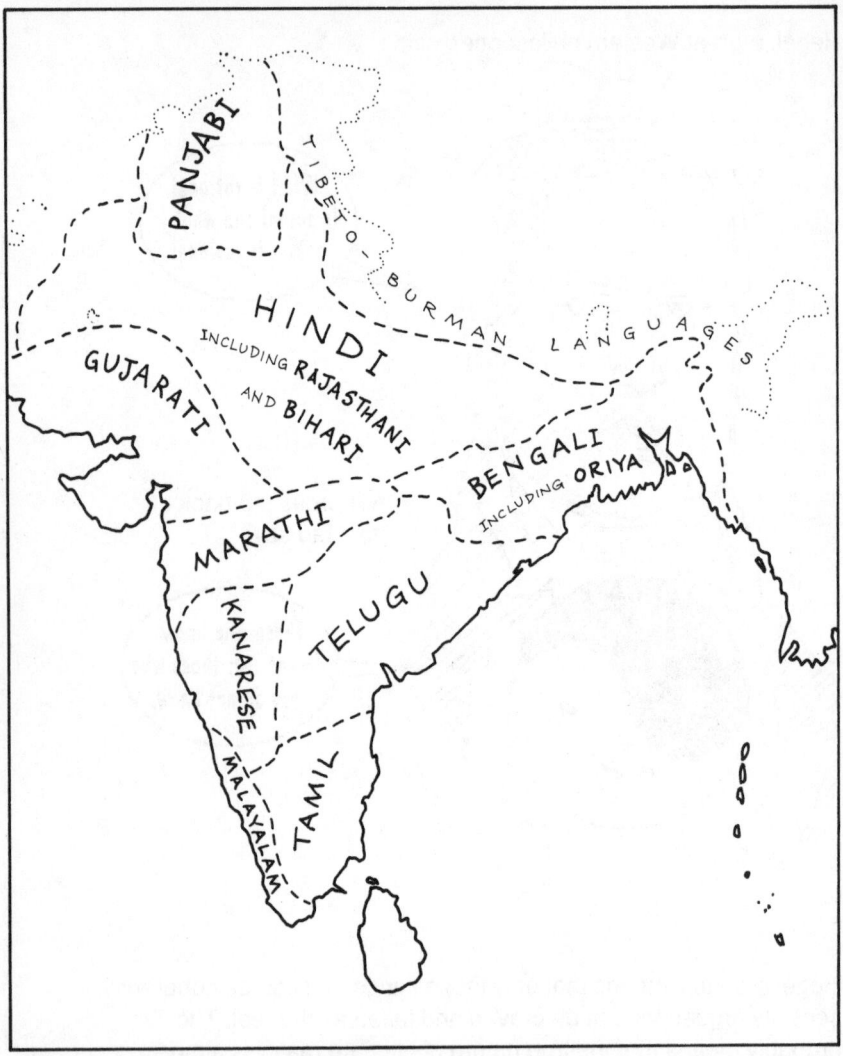

The Indian subcontinent is about half the size of the USA and in more modern times contains about one fifth of the human race. The various religions are represented in the following proportions:*

Hindus	216,000,000
Buddhists	11,000,000
Moslems	68,000,000

India: Race Divisions

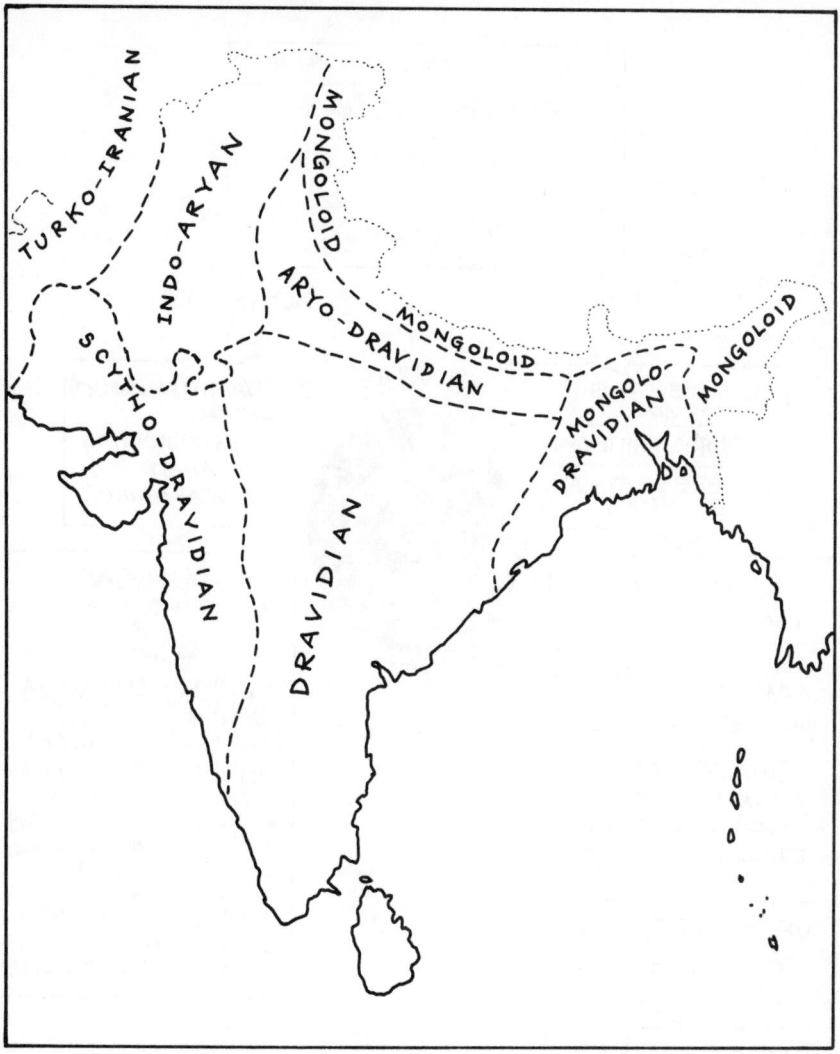

Animists	9,000,000
Christians	4,000,000
Sikhs	3,000,000
Jains	1,000,000
Parsees	101,800
Jews	21,000

**1921 census; later censuses show similar proportions.*

Indian Philosophy at a Glance

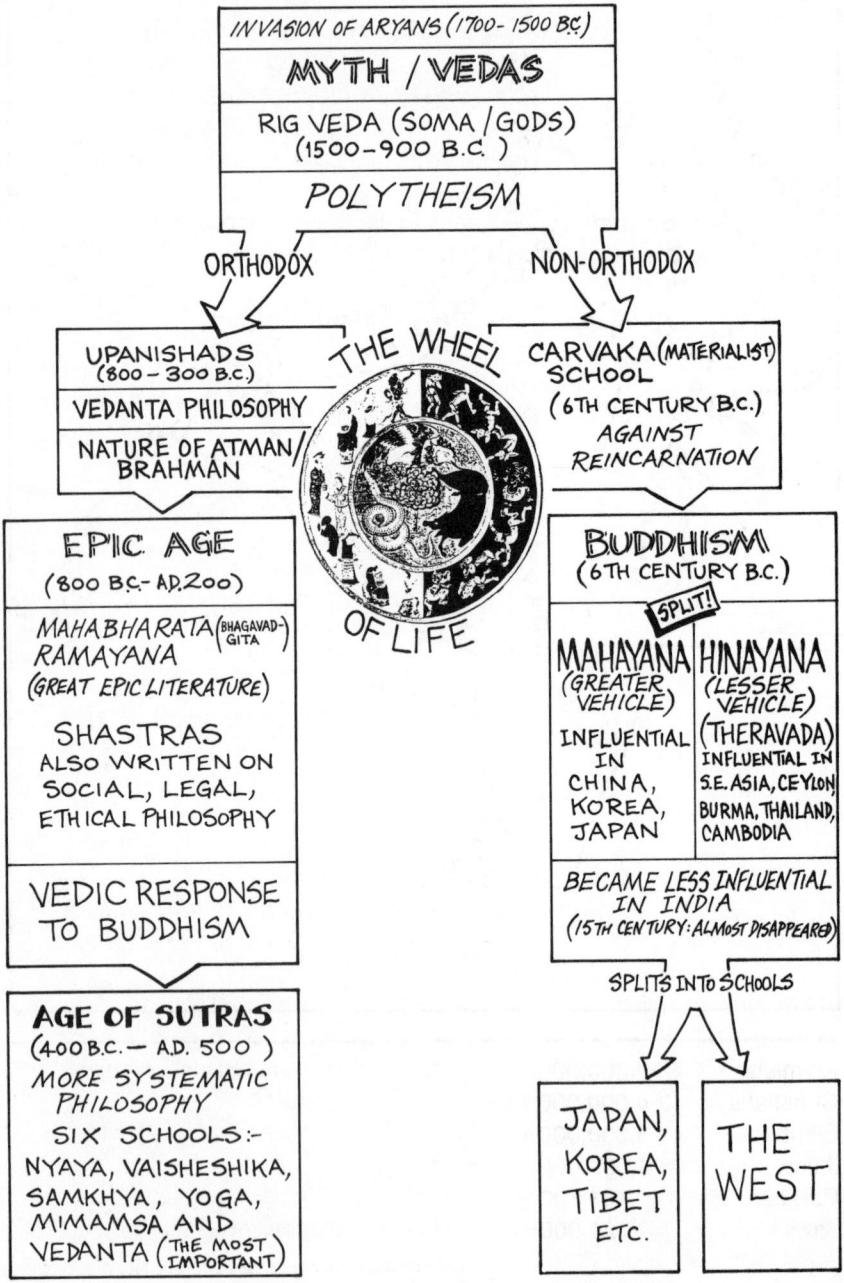

Some Key Characteristics of Indian Philosophy

1) History, myth, religion and philosophy constantly interact within a very long tradition.
2) There are two main schools, **Hindu** and **Buddhist**. The former accepts the authority of the ***Vedas***, the latter does not. There are still many similarities and overlaps, however, and both philosophies seek Enlightenment.
3) Almost all Indian philosophies seek Enlightenment through self-discovery (except the materialist schools which reject reincarnation).
THE KEY PHRASE IS:

Which means discovering your essence or true nature.
4) Within the main traditions, there are many schools of thought with a complex philosophical language that requires much study to understand fully. (We will just look at some of them.)
5) Most Indian philosophy is anti-empirical and concerned with an ultimate reality.
6) Hinduism does not have one founder and one truth but is a complex amalgam of many approaches.
7) Suffering, salvation and the ultimate reality are cornerstones of most Indian philosophizing.
8) In contrast with the absolute monotheism of Western religions, Hinduism is characterized by polytheism and pantheism – many gods, many voices.

Development of the *Vedas*

We need to begin probably some 5,000 years before Christ, when primitive ideas about natural gods began to form a coherent tradition.

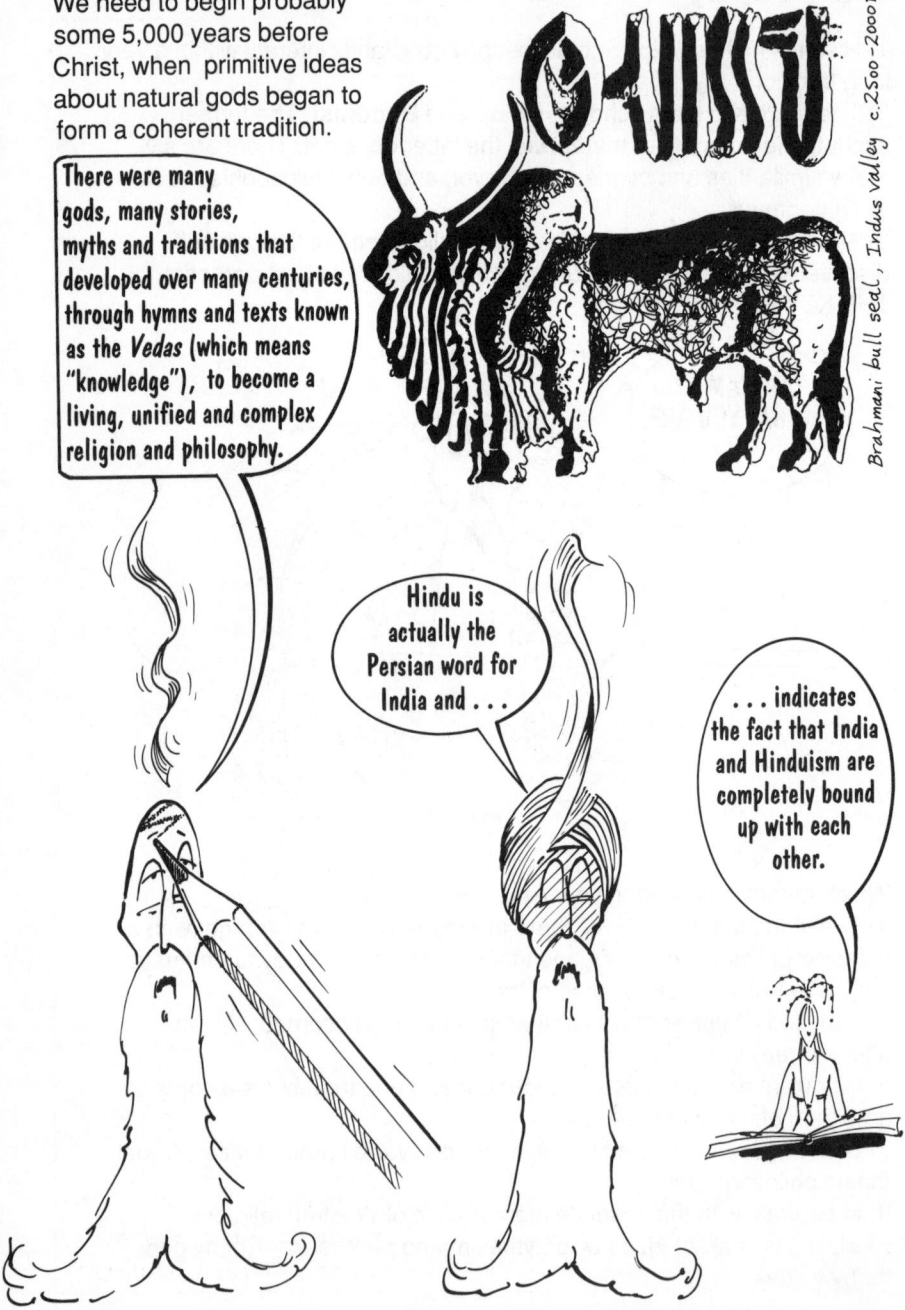

Despite all the complexities, we should remember one thing . . .

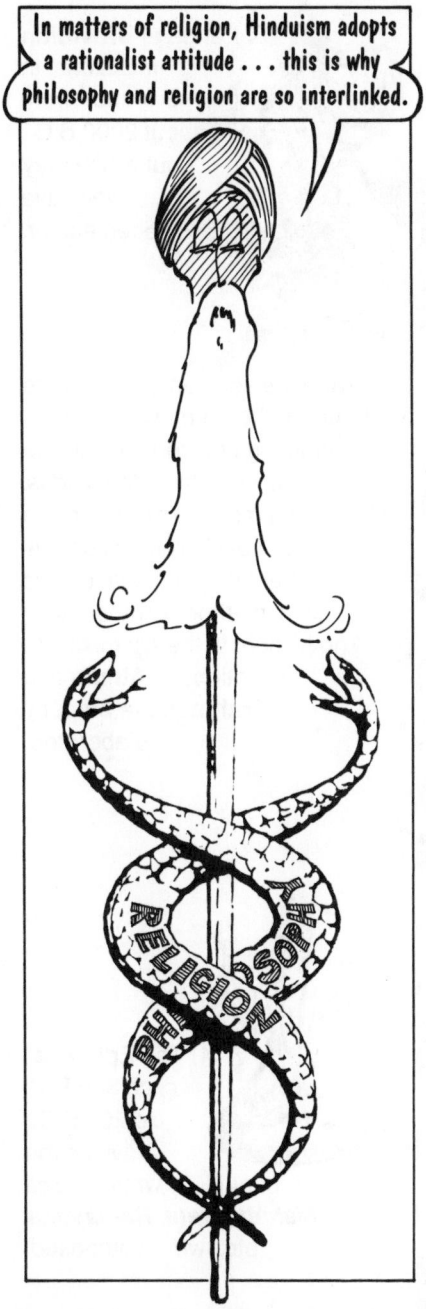

Indian philosophical and religious history can be roughly divided into seven main phases.

1) **Prehistoric** and mythic age – era of primitive religions.

2) Period of **Dravidian** invasions, in evidence from about 2000 B.C., but which may well have been earlier.

3) The **Vedic Period**, from about 1500 to 700 B.C., when the *Vedas* were composed. The ***Upanishads*** were also written during this era and are sometimes called the **Vedanta**, or the "end of the *Vedas*", summing up everything in the philosophy of the *Vedas*. Upanishad means something like "sitting down near", which suggests the teacher and pupil relationship as a method of transmitting knowledge. In the *Upanishads*, the notions of **Atman** and **Brahman** are properly elaborated.

SCENES FROM THE RAMAYANA

4) The **Epic Age**, circa 800 B.C. to 200 B.C., in which the beautifully written epics ***Mahabharata***, ***Ramayana***, etc., were composed.

5) **Age of Sutras**, circa 400 B.C. to A.D. 500. Philosophical thinking became organized through the composition of short **sutras** – or sayings – that could be easily memorized. Different schools developed.

6) **Age of Commentaries**, circa A.D. 400 to A.D.1700, in which the main schools were developed through rigorous commentaries on various sutras. **Sankara** is a major figure here.

7) The era of Renaissance and European influences. Internal influences included the **Bhakti** movements (which were devotional), Islam and Christianity, British imperialism, modernization and science, and of course the rise of Indian nationalism. The British ruled India for hundreds of years but probably never understood it.

Indian Diversity

The main thing about Hinduism and Indian philosophy is that they do not claim one master, one truth and one revealed wisdom, but **many**. This diversity is unusual in world religions and civilizations and is probably due both to the very mixed ethnic groups and invasions of India throughout its history and to its incredibly varied climate, geography and customs.

Because of the complex traditions of Indian philosophy, much of it can only be understood in relation to the other schools and debates, which is probably why there hasn't already been an ***Indian Philosophy for Beginners***!

Indian civilization is one of the seven wonders of the world. It may also be true that the great periods of human history are marked by a widespread access of spiritual energy derived from the fusion of national cultures with foreign influences. To put this another way . . .

The Aryan *Vedas*

Hinduism derived from ancient Vedic religions brought to India by people who called themselves **Aryans**. They arrived in India in waves between 2000 and 1000 B.C. The *Vedas* were transmitted in the form of cryptic poetry by word of mouth. There was no written language in India before the 4th century B.C. The ***Rig-Veda***, the oldest of them all, was created between 1500 and 900 B.C., which makes it older than any other text of philosophy or religion.

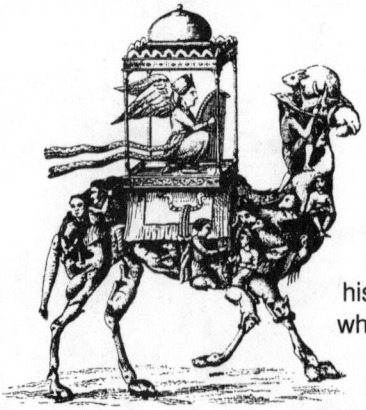

So we do not have much hard history to go by when discussing these early times.

Karma and the Caste System

We do know that from the earliest Vedic times there developed a caste system in India which was specific to it.

The caste system is a highly structured set of rules about which social group you belong to, and who you can talk to, marry, work with and so on. Which group you are in depends on your previous lives, how good you'd been and therefore the state of your **karma**. If you are a "lowest of the low", it must be because of the effects of your previous lives.

Basically it was thought up by the Aryans when they invaded India and called all the locals a load of "**Dasas**" (slaves).

A Karmic Hierarchy

At the top of the pile were the **Brahmans** (priests) and at the bottom were the **Sudras**, or servants. In between were the warrior-nobles (**Ksatriyas**) and the merchant farmers (**Vaisyas**). There are many sub-castes and the **Untouchables**, who are completely outside everything.

The notion of karma is a rather difficult philosophical concept we must come back to.

It is not at all clear that the caste system was supported by religion, by the scriptures, by all Brahmans, or by many groups within society. Its rigidity was often broken, sometimes even by the formation of new castes.

GANESH
The truth is that Indian culture is so ancient, so religious and so complex that it defies Western attempts to explain it rationally, which is the only way the West knows how to do it. To be spiritual is not to reject reason but to go beyond it.
But why are there so many gods and so many seemingly different approaches to understanding the world?
Because of our history, which is long, complex and interrupted by invasions, we have many religions, many gods and many philosophies. Hinduism combines them all. But there is just one way of realizing that man's true nature is within rather than without, however you express this.

So can I say that Buddhism, Hinduism, different kinds of Yoga, Bhakti, Vishnu, Jaina philosophies and all of these different schools all express a basic philosophical idea?
As the great sages say, Yes and No, or not at all in some respects but in others, and in essence, perhaps.
All Hinduism of whatever variety goes back to the *Vedas*, and there is a Vedanta philosophy which lies at the heart of all Hindu approaches, so you see complexity and simplicity co-exist . . . Put simply, all Hindu and Buddhist thinkers say that **Avidya** (ignorance) is the source of our unhappiness and that **Vidya** (wisdom) and **Bodhi** (Enlightenment) are our salvation. That is a common agreement amongst all Indian thought.

The Big Question of Indian Philosophy
What is the True Self?
Or to put it even more simply . . .
Who am I?
This leads to endless complexity because answering the question turns out to involve everything in the Universe and a few gods.
Yourself
A loony
Uddalaka
An illusion
A reincarnation of a rabbit
A speck in the Universe
That's a real help . . .

THEREFORE ALL REALITY IS BRAHMAN. EVERYTHING THAT IS INDIVIDUAL IS ATMAN; ATMAN IS BRAHMAN.
What on earth does that mean? All reality is Brahman?
Everybody knows that . . . It's from the *Upanishads.*
What are the *Upanishads?*

The *Upanishads*

Sometimes called the Vedanta, "end of the *Vedas*", the *Upanishads* are the fullest philosophical expression of the most dominant strand within Hinduism. Mostly belonging to the eighth and seventh centuries B.C., we find in them the monotheism and monism that characterize Hinduism. In these texts, the full philosophical discussion of the nature of Atman and Brahman are first found. The authors of the *Upanishads* and their exact dates are unknown.

WHAT IS KEY IS THE IDEA OF A TRANSCENDENTAL REALITY WHICH IS ALL-INCLUSIVE, BUT NOT A PERSONAL GOD.

that Indian philosophy has, from the very earliest times, been concerned with seeking self-enlightenment through the search for identity.
This search has been a process in which philosophy and religion have always been combined.
Seeking salvation has always meant searching for the higher, or ultimate reality, which lies behind worldly appearances.
BRAHMAN-CREATIVE, PRESERVATIVE & DESTRUCTIVE
More simply, Indian philosophy was not a philosophy of the mind but a philosophy of life in which you had to live the problem of trying to find deliverance.

I've been living the bloody problem for thirty years! I've run 20,000 miles trying to find the answer to the question of why my life is wall-to-wall suffering.
Isn't it because of what you did in a previous life? All that reincarnation stuff?
OK, so the wheel of life means we always live out our previous lives, but I'm always trying to get one step ahead and obey the rules about life's four goals . . .
TO BE VIRTUOUS
TO EXPERIENCE PLEASURE
TO MAKE A LIVING & EVEN BE COMFORTABLE
TO DEVELOP SPIRITUAL AWARENESS
Welcome to Marlboro Country.
FFICIAL WARNING: Sages say that smoking mess s up your karma
Bastard sahib.

The 4 Stages of Life

Working out how to live occupied Indian philosophers for a very long time – what we call ethics or the problem of what is right or wrong. Orthodox Indians came up very early on with a belief in the four stages of life, described as **student**, **householder**, **forest-dweller** and **hermit**.

These are known as **Asramas** or "rest-stops" which lead to the most important, spiritual awakening, for which one has to become a hermit.

These stages are not meant literally. You don't have to go and live in the forest.

But they correspond to patterns of searching for development and Enlightenment.

For example, the forest-dweller stage relates to holy men seeking the relative seclusion of the forest to contemplate and meditate.

The Student Stage

This involves a period of intense, disciplined study, mainly of the *Vedas*.

The Householder Stage

The Forest Dweller

The Final Stage

The aim of this phase is to develop **Moksha** or spiritual awareness. To do this, one must be entirely focussed on the higher reality and avoid all contact with everyday life. This kind of Eastern philosophy is sometimes accused of being anti-world and ascetic.

TO FIND THE ABSOLUTE REALITY IS NOT ANTI-WORLDLY BUT A SEARCH FOR TRUTH OR MOKSHA.

I will tell you three things which you must understand. 1) The ultimate reality which lies at the heart of the Universe is called Brahman. All gods and all things are simply manifestations of one ultimate being – Brahman.
2) He is Brahma, he is Shiva, he is Indra, he is the supreme, the changeless reality. He is Vishnu, he is the primal energy. He is Brahman.
3) Atman is Brahman. Therefore Tat tvam asi. THAT YOU ARE. Your true essence is absolute reality!
I need to take that one away and think about it.

Karmic Calamity: Women

In case we get too carried away with the brilliance of ancient thought, we should remember that, rather like many Western philosophers, many Veda thinkers saw women as a lower order of being. This was connected to the idea of trying to free oneself from earthly things and desires.

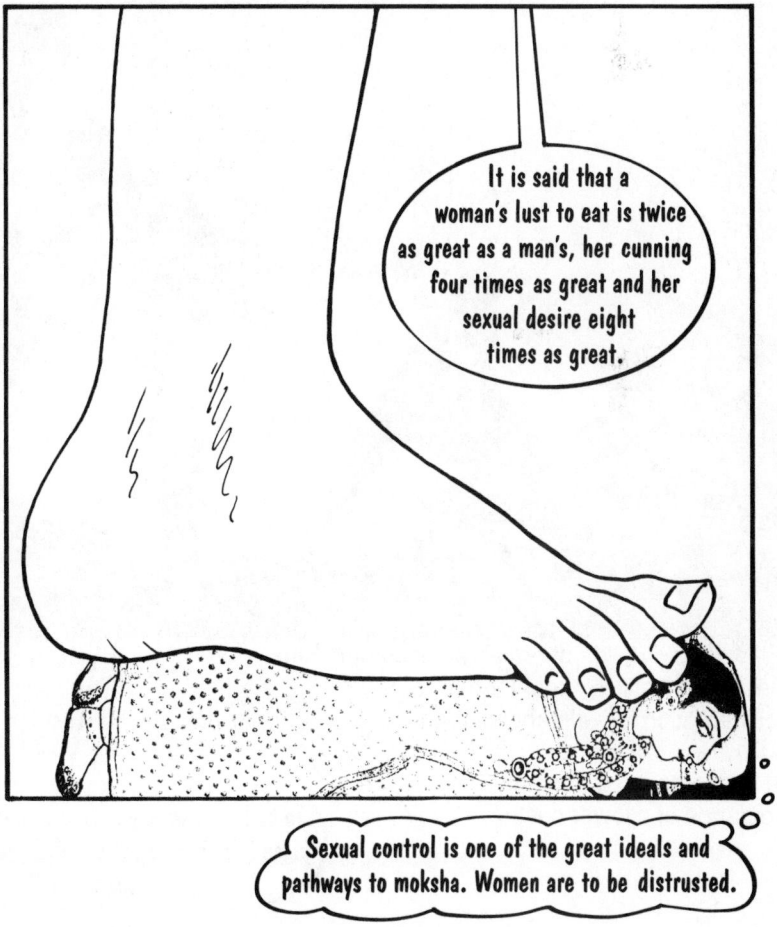

Some of the early Hindu rules about women . . .

1) A female should marry a male three times her age. An ideal age was 8 for the girl and 24 for the man.

2) A girl should marry before her first menstruation, otherwise she was likely to run sexually rampant.

3) Women should not be independent but under the rule first of their fathers, then their husbands, and if their husbands should die, their sons.

4) For women, to fulfil their **Dharma** is to be subservient.

5) Widows should not remarry, but commit **Sati**. Being burnt alive guaranteed blissful reincarnation for wife and husband.

6) A woman must not marry someone of a lower caste.

One of the more amusing practices that grew out of the idea of avoiding earthly distractions was . . .

The *Kamasutra*

Although the Upanishadic idea of turning away from the world is a strong one, there is another Hindu saying.

The ***Kamasutra*** is the well-known manual on the sensual art of love-making and accompanies much erotic art in Hindu temples. What are we to make of this seeming contradiction?

Hinduism does not completely suppress eroticism. It claims to confront and then supersede it by spiritual enlightenment.

Some Basic Principles of Vedanta Philosophy

Dharma means law or truth, and also maintenance. The whole Universe is governed by dharma. It covers everything and everybody, from gods to animals, and the ethical conduct of everyone within it. It can also mean the principle of existence. Within the universal framework of moral order, priority is given to the absolute necessity of virtue. Dharma demands that we fulfil our duty in accordance with our specified role – what could be seen as our caste position.

The moral codes derived from dharma can be seen as the ritualization of everyday life.

Dharma must be fulfilled or denied by each individual alone.

Moksha basically means genuine spiritual awakening, or the true Enlightenment. It also means liberation from the endless cycle of birth and death (samsara).

This is the aim towards which all the different pathways lead, and what the Buddhists call **Nirvana**. Trying to state clearly that nature of moksha is one of the great philosophical debates within the Indian tradition.

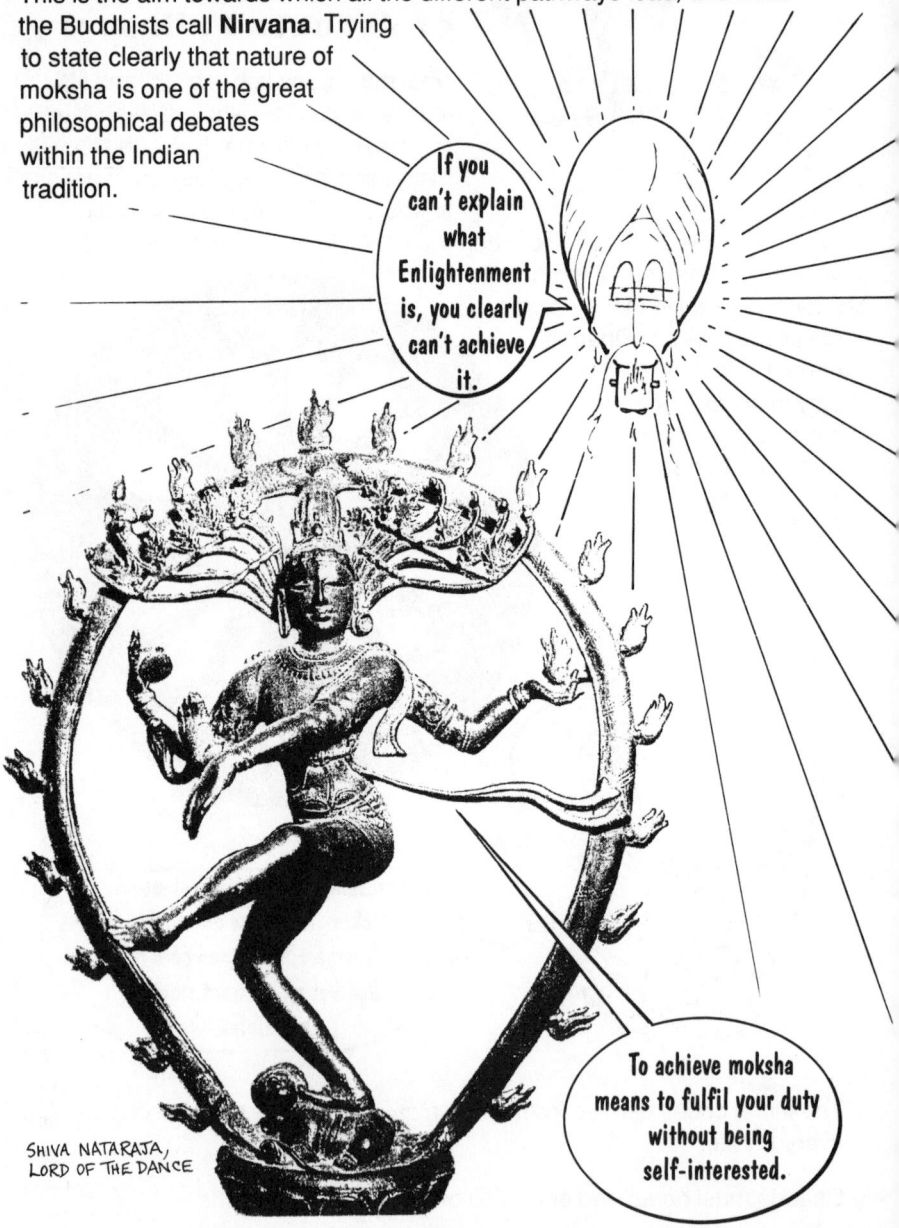

Karma

This is one of the most difficult ideas for Westerners to appreciate, but it is central to all discussions of Indian philosophy.

Although the wheel of samsara, of birth and death, sounds like a universal force, the idea of karma is one that implies individual responsibility.

KARMA ALSO MEANS ACTION OR DEED AND IT IS THE NEGATIVE AND POSITIVE CONSEQUENCES OF ALL OF OUR ACTIONS THROUGHOUT ALL OF OUR LIVES.

Your karma is the effect of your previous actions balancing the possibility of your future. Your karma is yourself.

PREVIOUS ACTIONS

As you live, so you accumulate karma.

Your reincarnation is a product of your karma. Karma is universal justice and a universal truth.

Karma implies transmigration of the spirit and the need ultimately to achieve moksha. It is the law of the Universe.

Even as a calf finds its mother among a thousand cows, an act formerly done is sure to find the perpetrator.

Samsara is the flow of change in all things, or the wheel of life, death and rebirth. Again, an idea which is very alien to Western thinking.

Samsara is the prison in which suffering and pain are the norm, and from which escape must be through many lifetimes and the accumulation of karma. Moksha, or Enlightenment, only comes to the few. Only through the ultimate realization of one's true nature, or Atman, does one escape samsara.

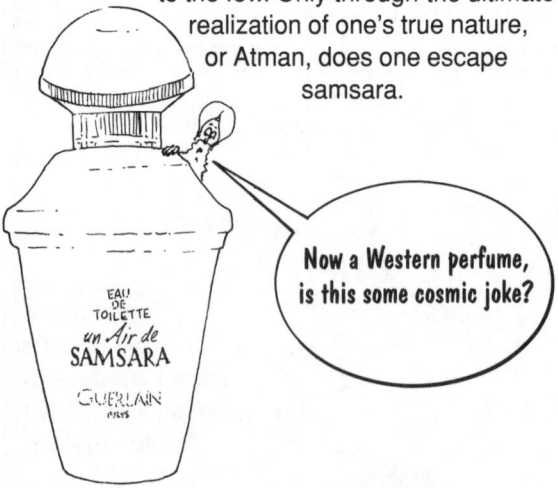

The *Bhagavad-gita*

This text is very influential and embodies the ideas of dharma in action. ***Bhagavad-gita*** literally means "sung by the lord". It is set within the wider framework of the ***Mahabharata***, a drama of two warring families, in which many of the philosophical ideas are given concrete realization through the action of the characters. Its 90,000 couplets are often memorized. The central part of the *Bhagavad-gita* concerns **Arjuna** who is about to enter battle but who is racked by doubt about his moral position. His charioteer, **Krishna**, the god in disguise, replies to his uncertainties and in so doing explains much of the notion of dharma.

Much of the poem is Krishna's exposition concerning death, reality, duty, action and ultimate understanding.

Elements of the *Bhagavad-gita*

The idea of the **Avatar** – a human intermediary between the gods and mortals. Krishna is both human and divine, a manifestation of the all-pervasive Brahman and of dharma. Thus a moral code, a philosophical idea and a notion of divinity are all expressed within a narrative framework that is comprehensible to all.

The *Bhagavad-gita* is therefore a model for understanding the philosophical ideas inherent in Vedanta schools. The Vedanta schools all argue the monistic view that all is Brahman.

The Sutra Period and the Six Schools

Called the Sutra period because many of the philosophical ideas that were around at the time were systematized in **sutras** – short sayings that could be easily remembered.

Six Orthodox Hindu Schools		
School	*Founder*	*Text*
Nyaya	Gautama	*Nyaya Sutras* (*c.* 3rd century B.C.–2nd century A.D.)
Vaiseshika	Kanada	*Vaiseshika Sutras* (*c.* 3rd century B.C.–*c.* 100 A.D.)
Samkhya	Kapila (*c.* 7th century B.C.)	*Samkhyapravacana Sutra*
	Isvarakrsna	*Samkhya Karika* (*c.* 3rd century A.D.)
Yoga	Patanjali	*Yoga Sutra* (*c.* 2nd century B.C.)
Mimanisa	Jamuni	*Purva-Mimanisa Sutra* (*c.* 400 B.C.)
Vedanta	Badarayana	*Brahma Sutra* (4th-2nd century B.C.)

The expression "**Darshana**" is used, which means "point of view" and signifies a sense of different philosophical approaches. However, the interpretation of these short sayings was not always clear, and thus the seeds of disputation and argument were laid.

The sutras became the basis of the later commentaries – all debate has to start with them. Wide differences existed between the philosophical schools . . .

The Nyaya and Vaiseshika Schools

Although still covering the same basic ground as other Indian philosophies, the **Nyaya** school advocated proper logical rules for reasoning. (Nyaya means something like "determining the right meaning".) In fact, they were very concerned with knowledge in general. Rather than just asserting things, the Nyaya school developed ways of arguing that are very similar to Western logic. From this kind of philosophy, arguments arose about the East's influence on the West.

Reasoning by SYLLOGISM was important both to the Nyaya and to Aristotle. The form of methodical reasoning adopted by the Nyaya was called the **Tarka**, and operated in five stages.

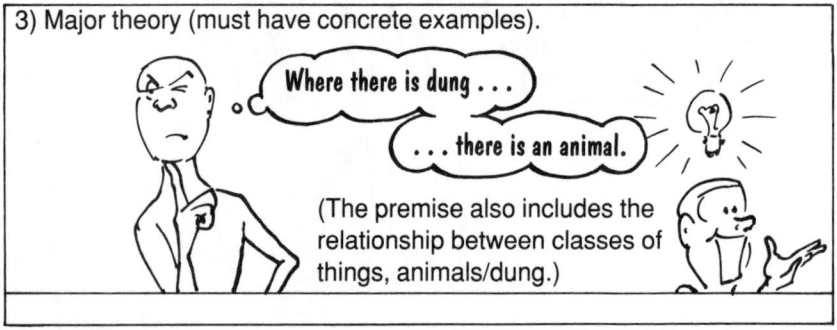

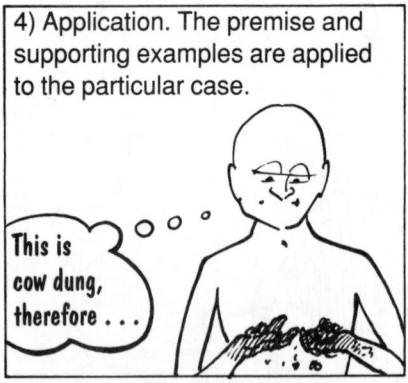

This formal method of reasoning also involves causality (cause and effect), which the Nyaya school were very keen on. The school was later divided into the Old and New Nyaya in the 12th century A.D. as more advances were made.

The Navya Nyaya (New Logic School)

Gangesa founded this influential branch of Eastern learning and logic in the 12th century A.D. Its main thrust was a philosophical analysis that was concerned with logical analysis.

Following on from the sense that what is real can be defined, they were very concerned with how one might define absence, or negation. Quite tricky, that one!

The Vaiseshika School

This school, which overlaps with the Nyaya, argued that physical reality is composed of invisible, indestructible atoms, of which there were four kinds. Again, there is a strange correspondence to ideas that the materialist Greek thinkers later put forward. The idea of this unseen structure of the Universe is used to support the idea that . . .

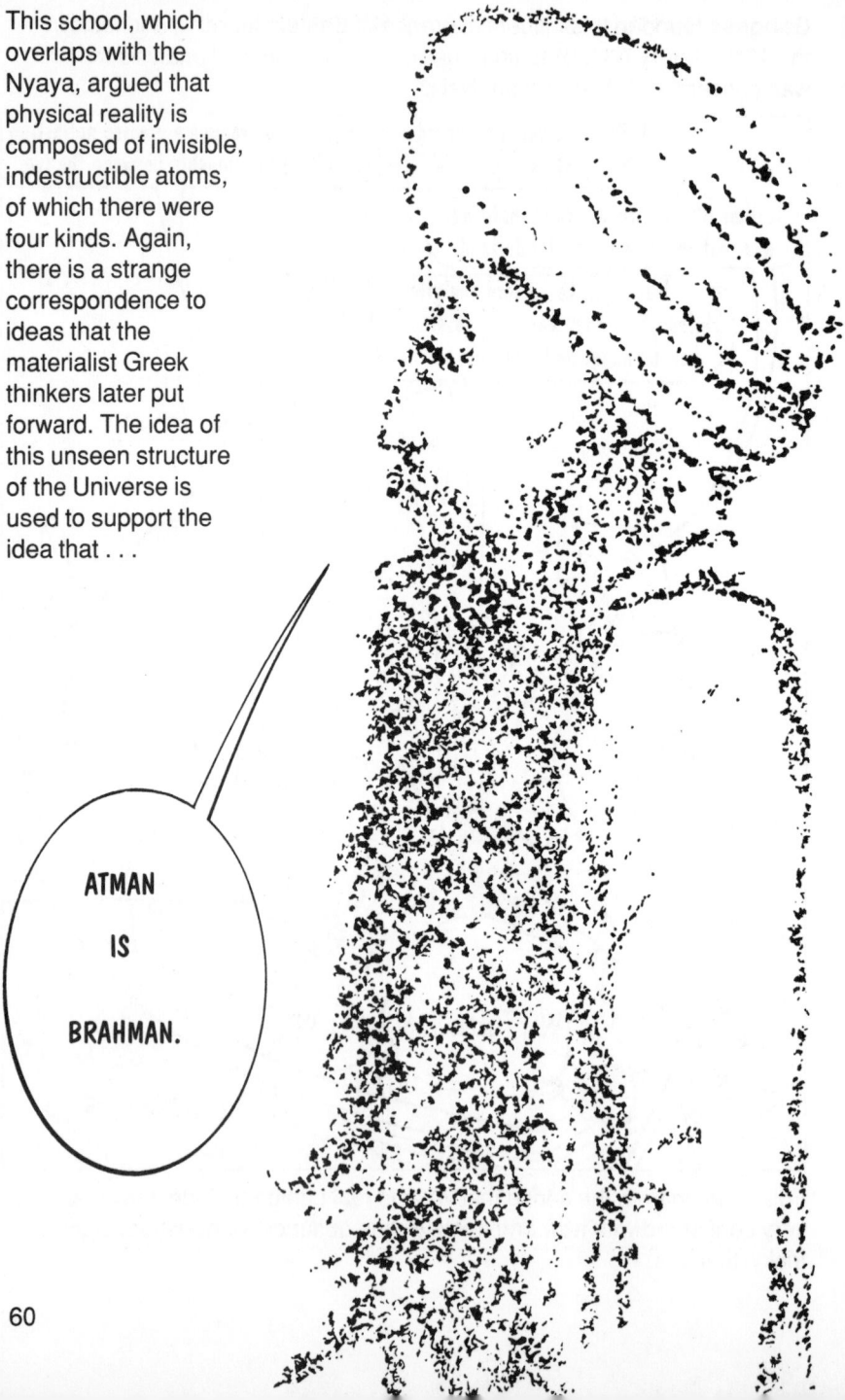

This combination of physics and metaphysics is an interesting one that reappears in modern Indian philosophy. Not everyone liked the school's line of reasoning about physical reality.

Samkhya School

Founded by **Kapila** who, it is thought, lived in the 7th century B.C. One of the most important schools in Eastern philosophy which advocates an interesting and quite complicated dualistic vision of the Universe.

Purusha and Prakriti

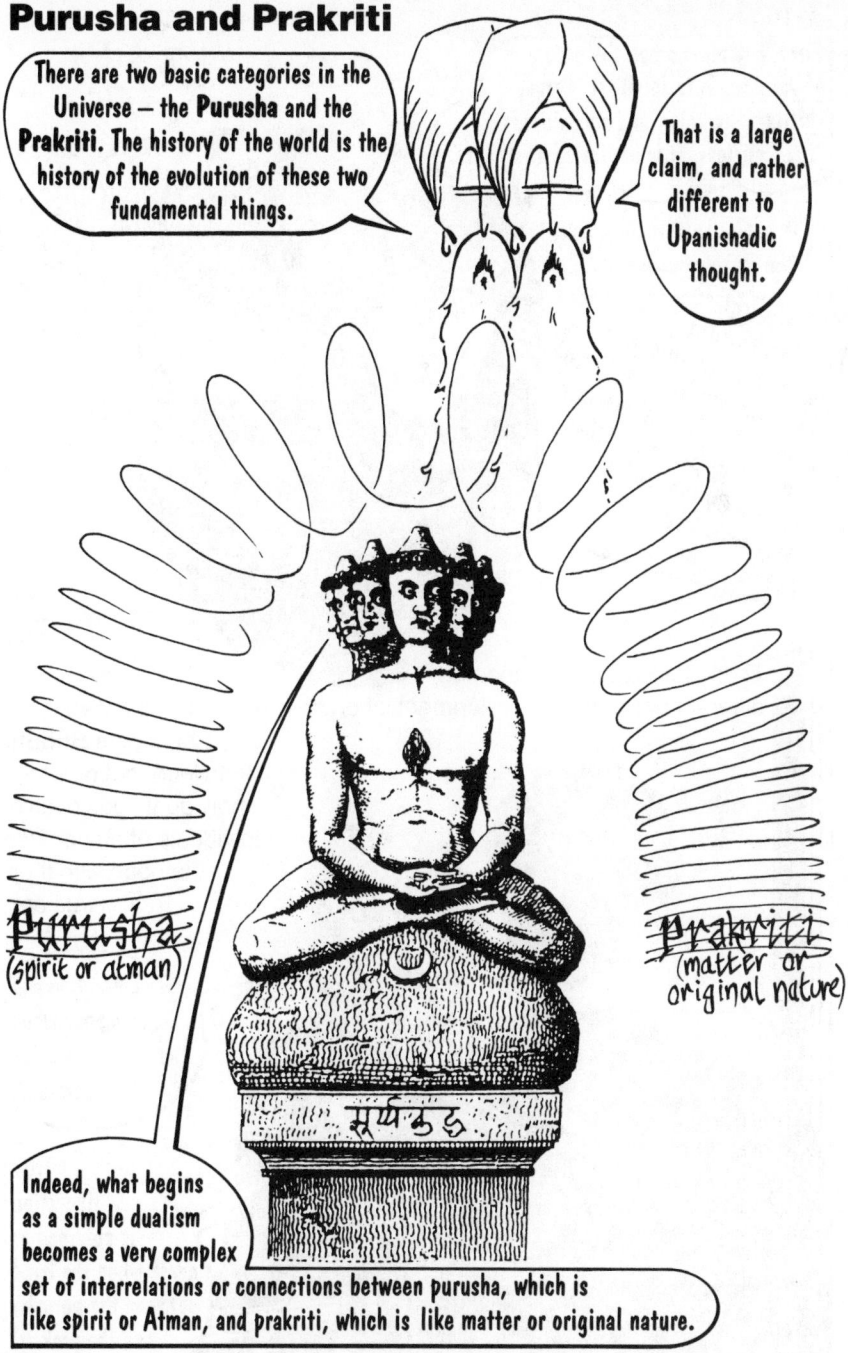

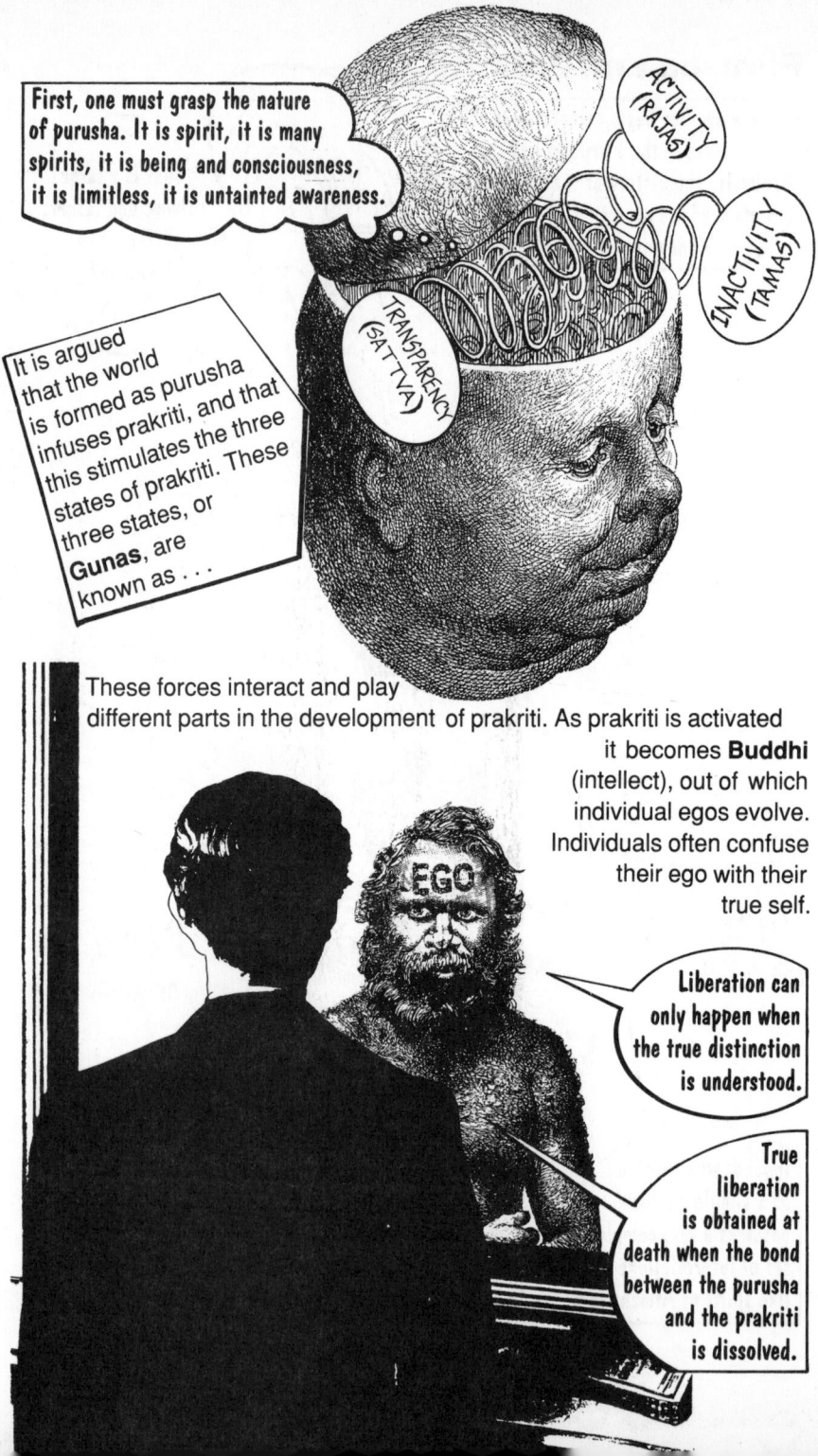
First, one must grasp the nature of purusha. It is spirit, it is many spirits, it is being and consciousness, it is limitless, it is untainted awareness.
ACTIVITY (RAJAS)
INACTIVITY (TAMAS)
TRANSPARENCY (SATTVA)
It is argued that the world is formed as purusha infuses prakriti, and that this stimulates the three states of prakriti. These three states, or **Gunas**, are known as . . .
These forces interact and play different parts in the development of prakriti. As prakriti is activated it becomes **Buddhi** (intellect), out of which individual egos evolve. Individuals often confuse their ego with their true self.
EGO
Liberation can only happen when the true distinction is understood.
True liberation is obtained at death when the bond between the purusha and the prakriti is dissolved.

The Samkhya school also believe strongly in causation, do they not? How does this fit in?
You mean that they argue for cause and effect and for the indestructibility of matter?
Exactly. It is known as the theory of the existent effect, which means that they imply that in the cause of all things the effect already exists.
Doesn't this mean that in some mysterious way the cause of something pre-exists its effect, even though they are distinct things?
Look, take a jar of clay. The jar is the clay but then it is not the lump of clay, clear?

Yoga School

This school is similar to the Samkhya school philosophically, except that a personal God is seen as the mover and shaker of the Universe. In **Yoga**, the search for the true self is both mental and physical. Philosophy and action are combined into a practice which seeks harmony.

One attempts to reach a state of "untainted" knowledge (or Enlightenment) by abandoning the pull of the mind and the body.

The Yogic tradition of disciplined meditation is a matter-of-fact, practical system for achieving Enlightenment. Rather than Enlightenment through knowledge, Yoga seeks to escape from prakriti into pure being (or purusha). The aim is to seek true reality. There are eight ascending steps in the discipline which lead to the **Samadhi** (highest state).

This is a very structured approach, which has also caught on in the West (probably because it is a brilliant way of relieving stress).

Advaita-Vedanta School

Vedanta means the "end of the *Vedas*" and **Advaita** means philosophical **monism**, or the idea that reality is one thing, not divisible. In the person of **Sankara** this notion was fully developed around the end of the 8th century A.D. This is certainly the most influential school in Hindu philosophy.

The Advaita school can be said to be based on three main texts:

Badarayana's

Understanding the nature of Brahman is obviously the key philosophical problem, and not one that is easily achieved.

The world exists, but only Brahman is real? Aren't those two things a bit contradictory?
Not at all. The world as we normally see it is still an illusion. For example what is that there?
It is a snake, of course.
That is just an illusion, but then there is actually a rope, if you look carefully.
The world is like the snake and Brahman is like the rope. One must look carefully.
So, you must understand that when we acquire true knowledge we can see that the world is just a manifestation of Brahman.
The world is neither real nor unreal. It is a form of appearance based on the nature of Brahman.

The relationship between the world and Brahman is clearly quite a tricky one and in fact sometimes the argument is that it is inexpressible, or **Maya**. It brings us back to the question of:

The answer is that without Brahman there can be no world, but of course Brahman does not depend on the nature of the appearance of the world. So, to make statements about Brahman means they must have an empirical form, but in one sense these are an illusion, like the snake was. Brahman can be viewed in two ways: as **Nirguna**, without characteristics, and as **Saguna**, with characteristics.

Sankara argued that Brahman and Atman are one, and that Brahman is the cause of the world, but that somehow the world is only a manifestation of its original cause.

Medieval and Later Indian Thought

Indian thought continued to develop, but always with reference back to the original texts and positions. **Ramanuja** (1056–1137) and **Madhva** (1197–1276) were two scholars who later put forward reinterpretations of the *Upanishads*. Ramanuja believed in what is called a **qualified nondualism**.

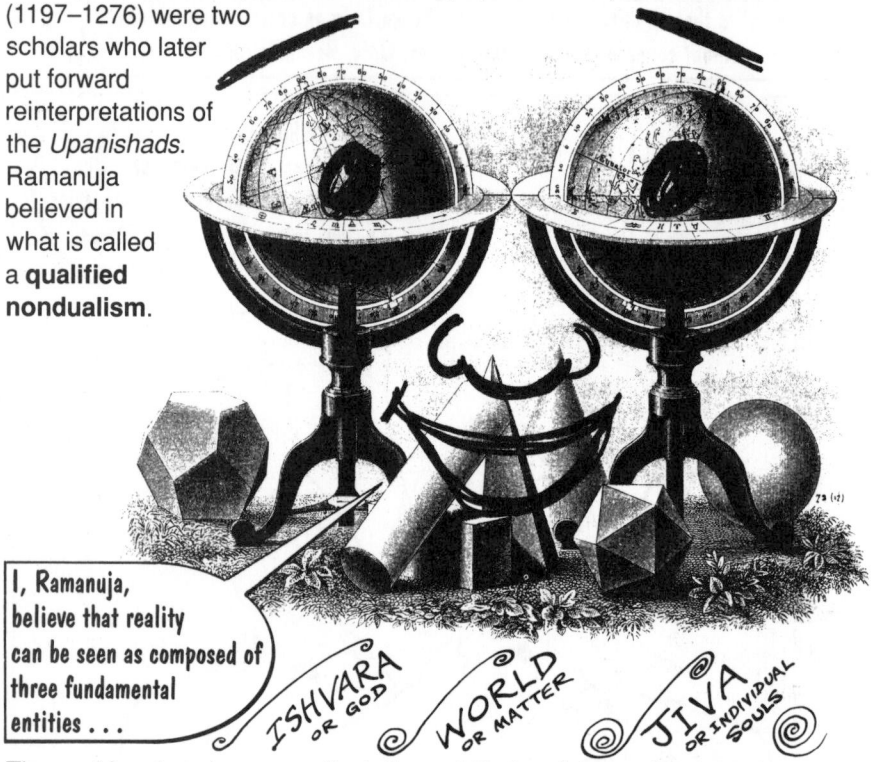

The world and souls are manifestations of God, or Ishvara (Brahman), but they are distinct from it. So he is arguing that God is everything, but that the body and the soul are attributes of God, they qualify God, but are distinct. His main point is that Brahman can only be known through its attributes, or in other words through the world.

Madhva (13th Century)

Madhva argued for the dualism of Brahman and Jiva (individual souls). He opposed Sankara's nondualism and said that all things are different.

Madhva views God as **Vishnu** and as completely transcendent, as the only self-sufficient reality on which everything else is reliant. His philosophical ideas were later utilized by the Bhakti devotional movements which approached God not through knowledge, but through simple devotion.

Jainism

This school was traditionally founded by **Vardhamana Mahavira** (599–527 B.C.). Its approach elevated an absolute respect for life, as well as the idea of non-violence or **Ahimsa**.

The most famous exponent of this view is **Mahatma Gandhi** (1869–1947). Ironically enough, he was violently assassinated by a Hindu.

The **Jaina** code of conduct was aimed, like Buddhism, at escaping from the endless wheel of life (samsara), and involved the Three Jewels:

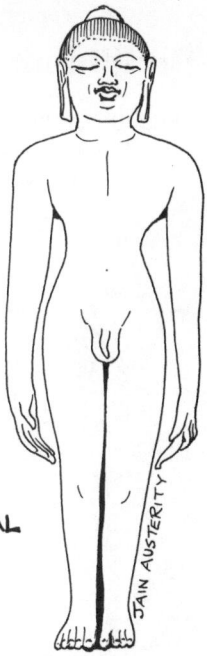

There were also five vows:

- NOT TO KILL
- NOT TO SPEAK UNTRUTH
- NOT TO STEAL
- CONTIN-ENCE
- RENUNCIATION OF ALL EXTERNAL PLEASURES & THINGS

The Jainist approach which involved non-violence, asceticism and an absolute respect for life, had a major influence in India in the medieval period. The extreme ascetics of the **Digambara** ("sky-clad") group practised nudity as an expression of complete detachment.

This never caught on in the northern provinces.

Buddhism

Although Buddhism is opposed to the philosophy of the *Vedas*, and to what it sees as its metaphysical abstractness, it is based in Hindu traditions. It is less strictly philosophical than many of the schools, being more concerned with practical liberation from suffering.

Buddhist teachings are based on what are called the Three Jewels of Buddhism: the **Buddha**, the **Dharma**, and the **Sangha**. The life of Buddha himself is the first jewel, and the story of his searching for truth forms the prime example of his teachings.

The Buddha

Buddha (otherwise known as **Siddhartha Gautama**) lived 536–476 B.C. and finally obtained Enlightenment sitting under a tree in the town of Bodh Gaya. His "awakening" led to the second jewel, the Dharma.

Buddha wandered about for forty-nine years after his "awakening", spreading the gospel and the idea of achieving "nirvana".

The Four Noble Truths

The Dharma is expressed by the **Four Noble Truths**, and the part known as the **Middle Way**, which sounds rather like what Aristotle called the Golden Mean. The Four Noble Truths are . . .

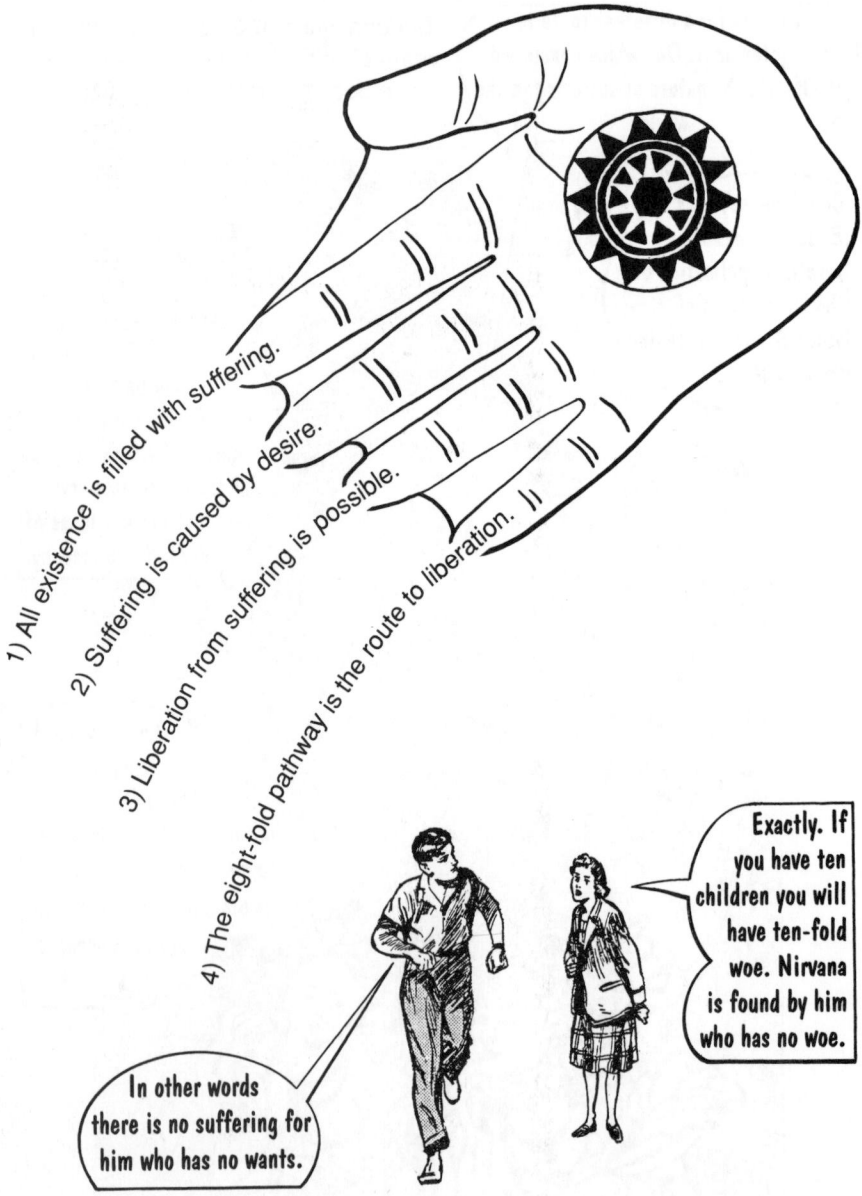

Buddhism avoided the ritual and élitism of Vedic approaches, teaching in the common languages of the day and supporting an egalitarian approach to Enlightenment.

Yet Buddhism didn't fare all that well in India itself, but became a very important force in many parts of Asia and the East, particularly China and Japan, which we'll come to later.

Differences between Buddhism and Vedic Thought

The Self in Buddhism

The orthodox schools of Hindu philosophy are all concerned with the nature of the self, and with the notion that Atman is Brahman. Buddhism takes a completely different line.

Buddhism asserts that there is no unique individual self. This philosophical position is very radical and, of course, difficult for Westerners to take on board.

The Buddhist Idea of Rebirth

The Buddhist philosophical position is based on the idea that there is a continuity, there are links from one existence to another, but that the "self" is an illusion created by the combination of mental and physical activities. Meditation is a way of approaching the mind as pure mind, to get past the illusion of self.

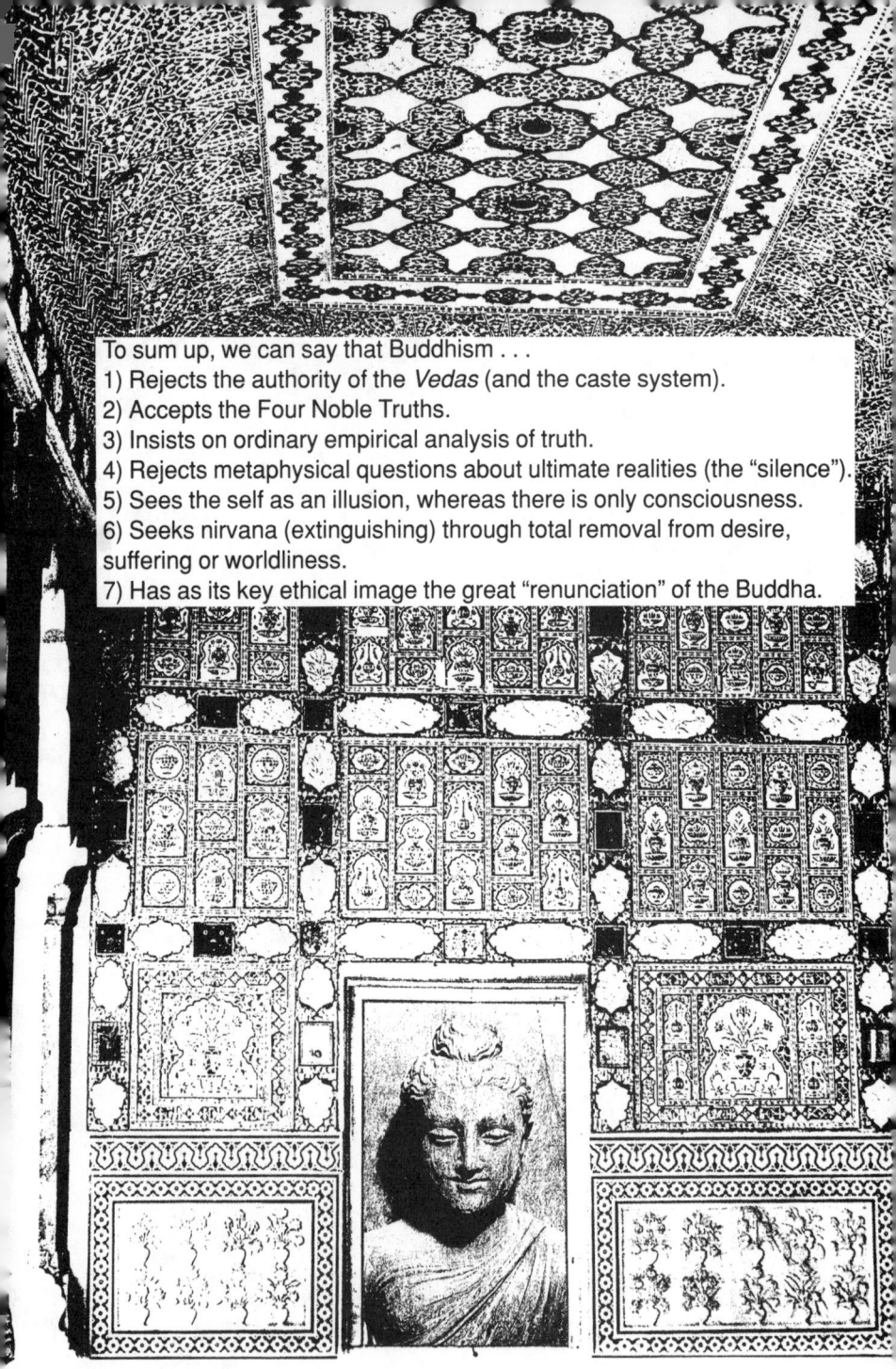

To sum up, we can say that Buddhism . . .

1) Rejects the authority of the *Vedas* (and the caste system).
2) Accepts the Four Noble Truths.
3) Insists on ordinary empirical analysis of truth.
4) Rejects metaphysical questions about ultimate realities (the "silence").
5) Sees the self as an illusion, whereas there is only consciousness.
6) Seeks nirvana (extinguishing) through total removal from desire, suffering or worldliness.
7) Has as its key ethical image the great "renunciation" of the Buddha.

The Spread of Buddhism from India

Buddhism had a great influence all over the Eastern world, and, in more modern times, in Western countries.

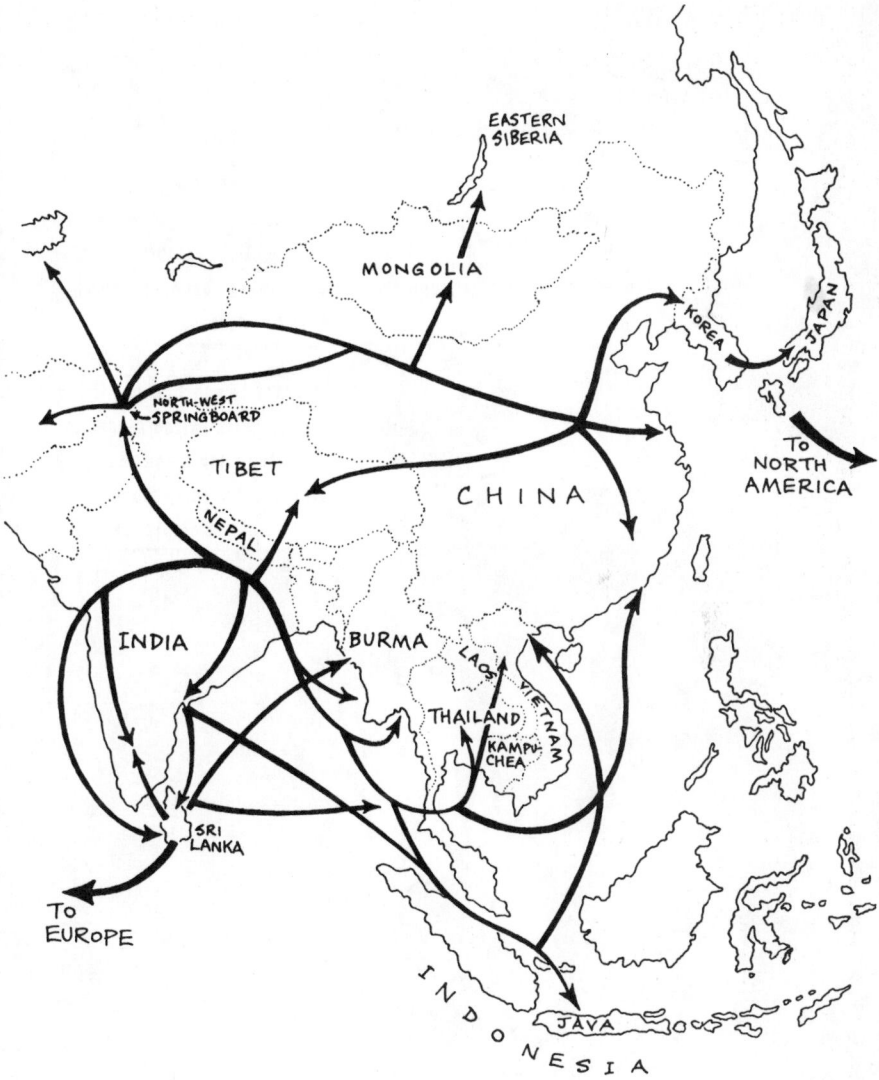

Throughout the many schools of Indian thought we have discussed, there have been consistent debates about the nature of reality and the many different approaches to explaining it.
Though the world is always changing, it has a unity and a meaning.
The great strength of our thought has been its quite extraordinary ability to combine the simple and the complex, the divine and the real, the active and the contemplative.

This has ensured its continuity . . .
. . . and may well be why it appeals more and more to Western minds who see the limitations of the secular rationalism of the West.
We will come back later to the problems of modernism, postmodernism and philosophical possibility, or moksha.

China and Philosophy

To consider China and its philosophy is to make another giant leap, because Chinese culture, although Eastern, is markedly different to Indian. What fundamentally distinguishes Chinese culture is its sense of harmony, interconnectedness, language and continuity. China has a cult of the Old in which tradition is everything.

Chinese Language

In discussing Chinese philosophy we first need to recognize that there is a real problem of translation. The Chinese language is nothing like the Western languages we are used to. Rather than an alphabet it uses characters (or ideographs) which are much less precise than a phonetic and grammatically organized language like Latin.

Chinese is a language much more allusive and dependent on context than Romance languages. It is not a language easily amenable to logical philosophy.

China's Culture

Chinese culture is one of the most ancient and self-contained we know of, and its longevity is one of the key features that mark it out as unique. Its philosophy, rather like Indian philosophies, shows a complexity and unity which incorporates many diverse veins and philosophical strategies that stretch over thousands of years. Unlike India, however, the gods do not loom large in early Chinese civilization.

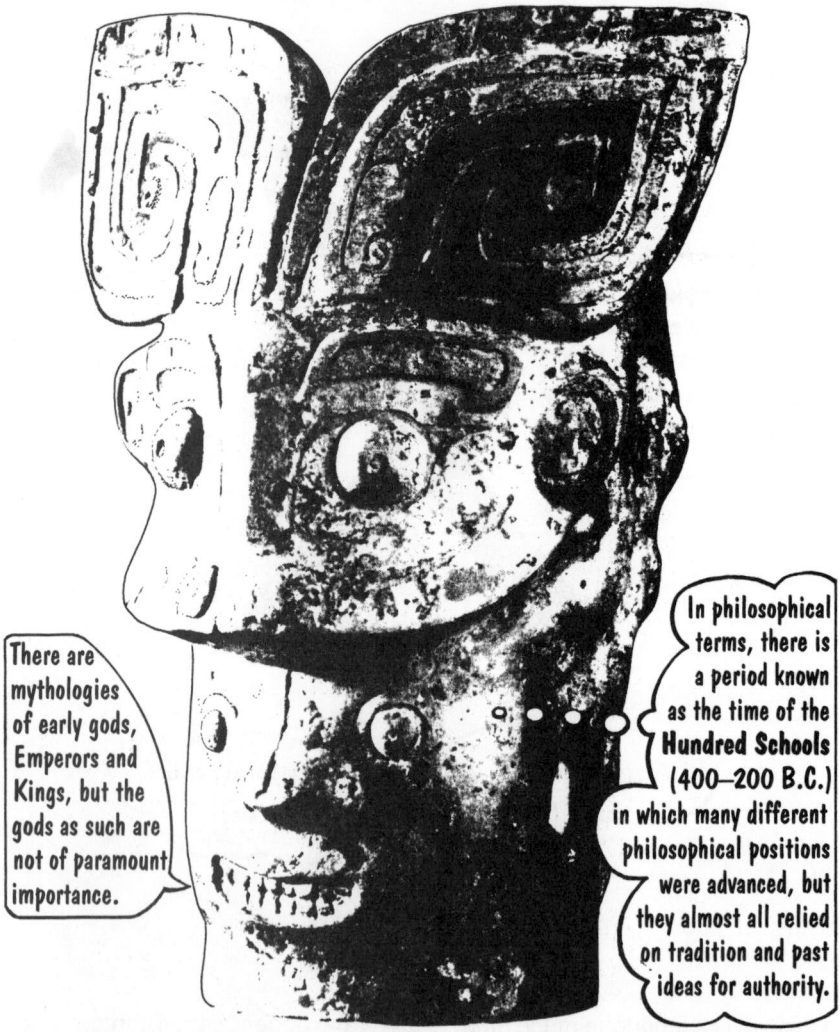

The oldest examples go back 3,000 years B.C. We have no idea whether they are entirely true, false or a mixture.

The Role of Philosophy

In Chinese culture, philosophy has played the role that religion plays in the West. What do we mean by this?

Simply that Chinese civilization has always assumed that everyone who has an education will naturally study and understand their traditional philosophies.

Chinese culture does not depend on the idea of a God to whom everyone is answerable, nor do its original myths talk about a supernatural creation. Chinese culture is secular and philosophical in the broadest sense.

From the earliest days of Chinese civilization, traditional ways of thinking were passed from generation to generation.

From the earliest times, Confucius had an idea of the man of virtue, the Gentleman (Chun-Tzu), and this defined an ethic, a mode of behaviour and a social order.

Chinese Civilization at a Glance

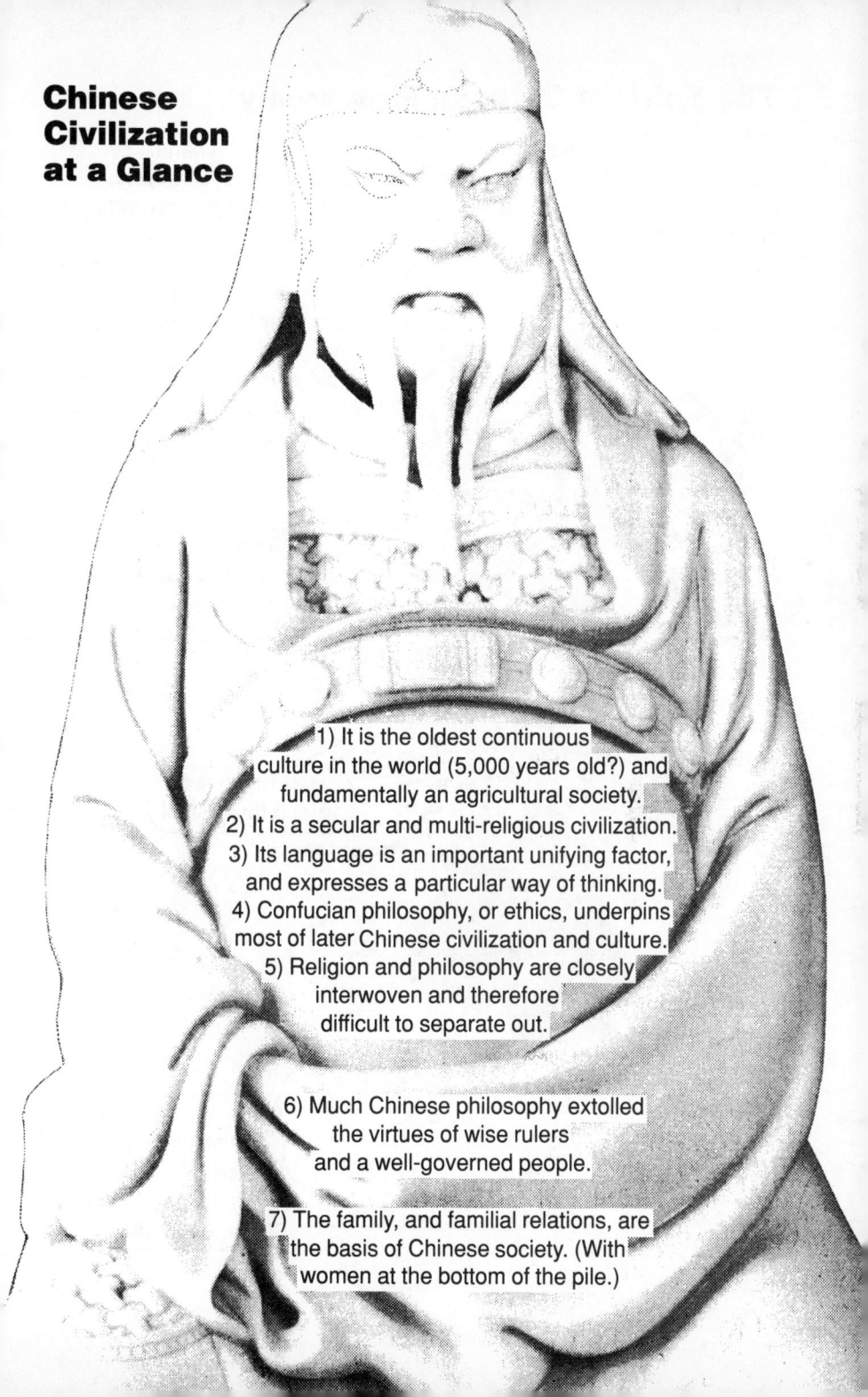

1) It is the oldest continuous culture in the world (5,000 years old?) and fundamentally an agricultural society.

2) It is a secular and multi-religious civilization.

3) Its language is an important unifying factor, and expresses a particular way of thinking.

4) Confucian philosophy, or ethics, underpins most of later Chinese civilization and culture.

5) Religion and philosophy are closely interwoven and therefore difficult to separate out.

6) Much Chinese philosophy extolled the virtues of wise rulers and a well-governed people.

7) The family, and familial relations, are the basis of Chinese society. (With women at the bottom of the pile.)

The Spirit of Chinese Philosophy

What then is the distinctive spirit of Chinese philosophy? A certain Dr. Fung, who wrote a very long ***Short History of Chinese Philosophy***, said that one of the recurring themes was a notion of "Sageliness within and Kingliness without".

To put it in the most general way, Chinese philosophy is down-to-earth. It is not concerned with God, or with absolute truth, but with the question of how to live properly on earth, with ethics, the principles of social living and government.

Main Stran of Chinese Thought

The Ancient Dynasties

There are many preconceptions in the West about China, many of them based on the strange reportings of Marco Polo and other Westerners who have imagined China in their travels. Even today we know little about Chinese history. The earliest period we have definite evidence for is the **Shang** dynasty (1766–1123 B.C.). When we reach the **Chou** dynasty (1122–256 B.C.), we reach the period of the greatest historical knowledge and also the Golden Age of Chinese philosophy.

The Four Phases

We can roughly divide Chinese philosophical history into four major phases.

Ancient Period (before 200 B.C.): Characterized by many competing (The Hundred) schools.
Middle Period (200 B.C.–A.D. 960): Confucianism, Taoism and the introduction of Buddhism.
Neo-Confucianism (960–1912): Reaction to Buddhism, renaissance of Confucianism.
Modern Period (1912–present): Arrival of Western thought, revival of Confucianism and Marxism.

Throughout it all, there is the deep sense of the self-contained continuity of China, or as Confucius put it . . .

Two Main Trends

The values of Chinese society grew out of the "value of agriculture", the family and the state that were based on these two things. There were two main trends, Taoism and Confucianism, which seem the opposite of each other but which constantly interact to produce the dynamic stability of Chinese thought.

The ***Book of Changes*** (***I Ching***) says:

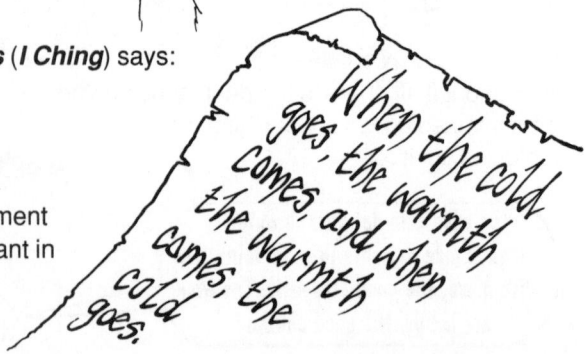

This sense of development and negation is important in both Confucianism and Taoism.

Chinese Humanism

Chinese philosophy was humanistic, by which we mean that it thought of man as being the centre of the Universe. In this sense, Chinese philosophy was very much this-worldly rather than other-worldly. However, if this were wholly true, it would be very difficult to explain why Buddhism became so popular in China. Buddhism is very concerned with leaving this world behind in achieving nirvana.

The First Scholars

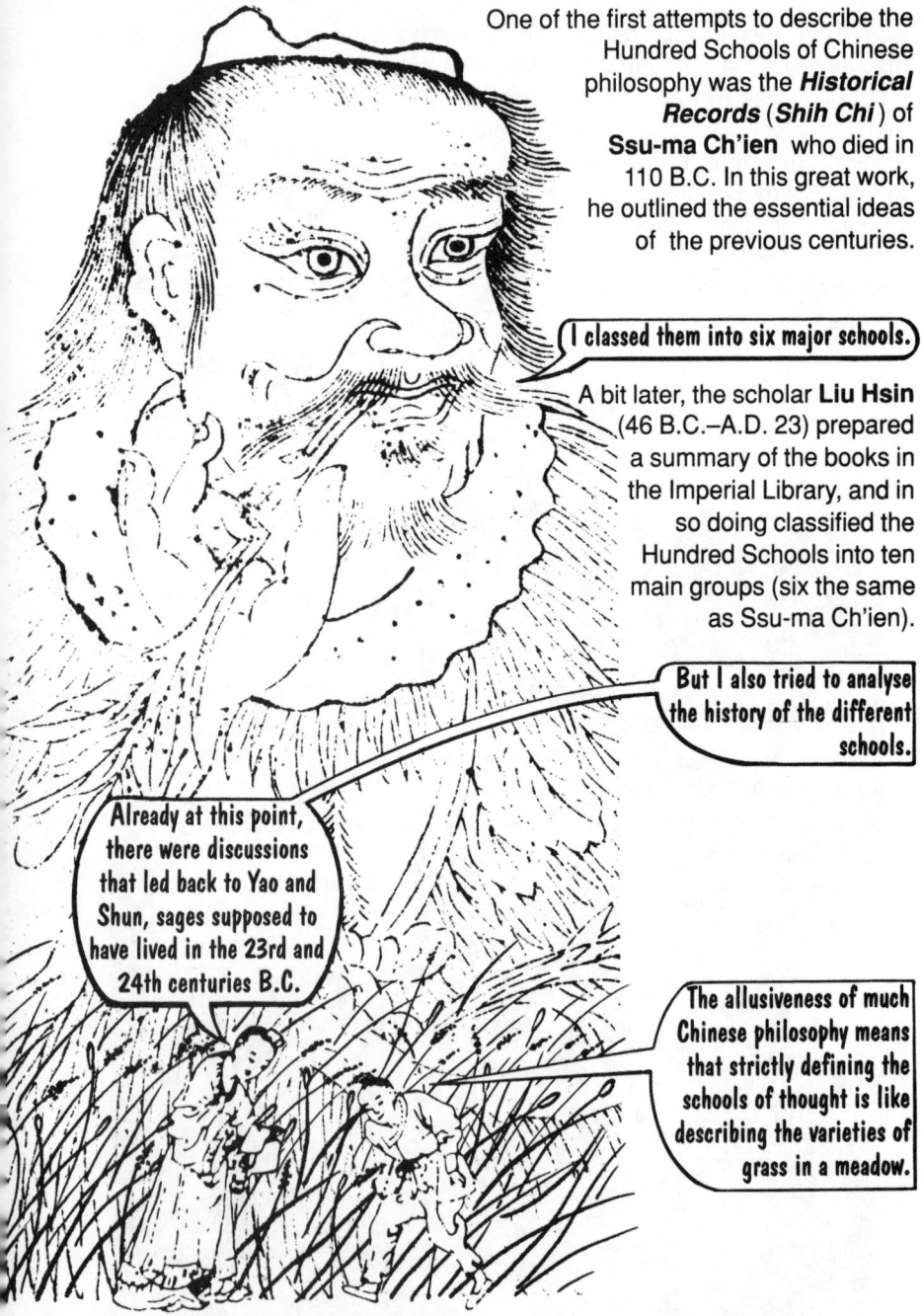

One of the first attempts to describe the Hundred Schools of Chinese philosophy was the ***Historical Records*** (***Shih Chi***) of **Ssu-ma Ch'ien** who died in 110 B.C. In this great work, he outlined the essential ideas of the previous centuries.

A bit later, the scholar **Liu Hsin** (46 B.C.–A.D. 23) prepared a summary of the books in the Imperial Library, and in so doing classified the Hundred Schools into ten main groups (six the same as Ssu-ma Ch'ien).

Interestingly, Liu Hsin sees the origins of the different schools in the functions of the officers of the Court, or in specific groups and their functions in society. It is almost a "sociological" approach.

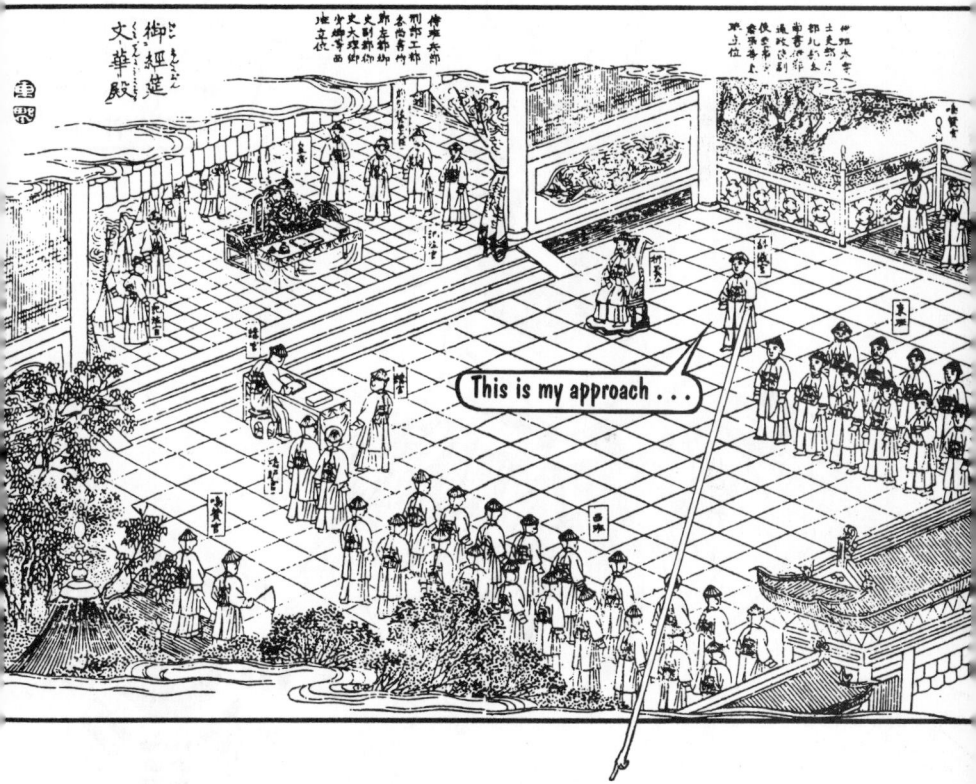

The **Ju** (Confucian school) had their origin in the literati.
The **Yin-Yang** school developed from the cosmologists.
The **Mohist** school had its origins in the knights.
Members of the **Taoist** school came from the hermits.
The **School of Names** came from the professional debaters.
The **Legalist** school came from the "men of methods" (politicians).

Ssu-ma Ch'ien's Divisions

The **Yin-Yang Chia** (Yin-Yang school). Deriving from ancient cosmology, it was concerned with the two basic principles which govern the Universe, now quite well known in the West.

Yin represents the passive female principle and **Yang** the active male. The two constantly interact to create all things and all development.

These ideas were later connected with the famous *I Ching* (*Book of Changes*) which described the cosmological principles of the Universe and elaborated them in ways that could be divined through patterns of hexagrams.

This basic idea has many consequences and runs throughout Chinese philosophy.

The Yin-Yang school and its ideas of the natural interplay of universal forces had very deep roots in Chinese popular culture.

Confucius

The second school is known as the **Ju Chia** (school of the literati), also known as the Confucian school, of whom **Confucius** (551–479 B.C.) was obviously the most important figure.

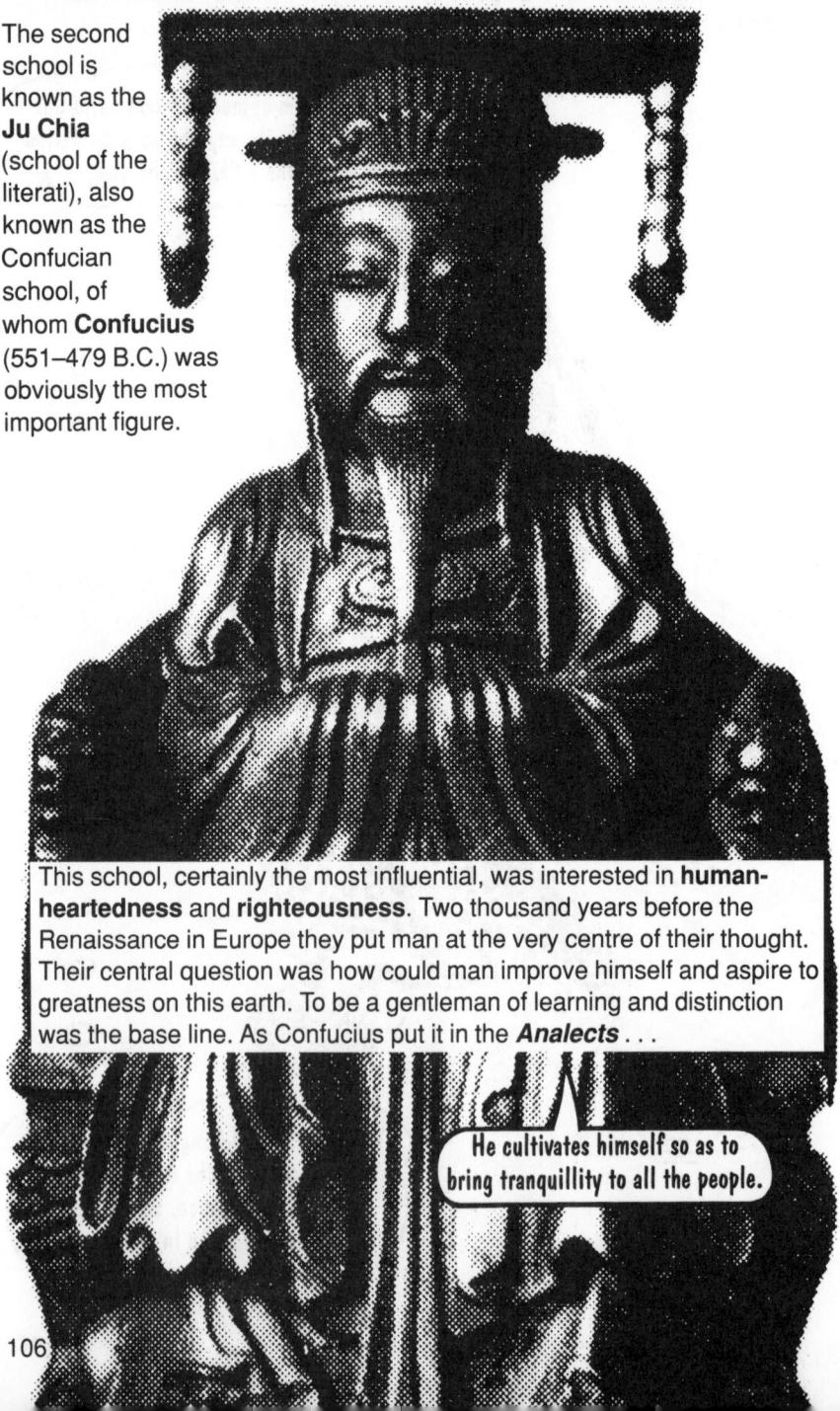

This school, certainly the most influential, was interested in **human-heartedness** and **righteousness**. Two thousand years before the Renaissance in Europe they put man at the very centre of their thought. Their central question was how could man improve himself and aspire to greatness on this earth. To be a gentleman of learning and distinction was the base line. As Confucius put it in the ***Analects*** . . .

The philosopher sage **K'ung Fu-Tzu** lived about 2,500 years ago and has probably had more influence than any other philosopher in world history. "Confucius" is the Latinized name given to him later. We know little of his real life and are not certain that he actually wrote his famous *Analects* (sayings). The first biography of Confucius was not written until some three hundred years after his death, so its accuracy must be questioned. Certainly, there is a body of knowledge and teachings that are ascribed to Confucius. **Mencius**, who lived a hundred years after the sage and who founded the tradition that bears his name, said of him . . .

It is said that Confucius worked in Government, and later in his life taught privately. It seems probable that he was one of the first in Chinese history to teach large numbers of students privately (probably thousands), and many of them went on to become famous scholars and thinkers.

The *Six Classics*

The ***Six Classics*** correspond to the liberal arts (or **Liu Yi**).

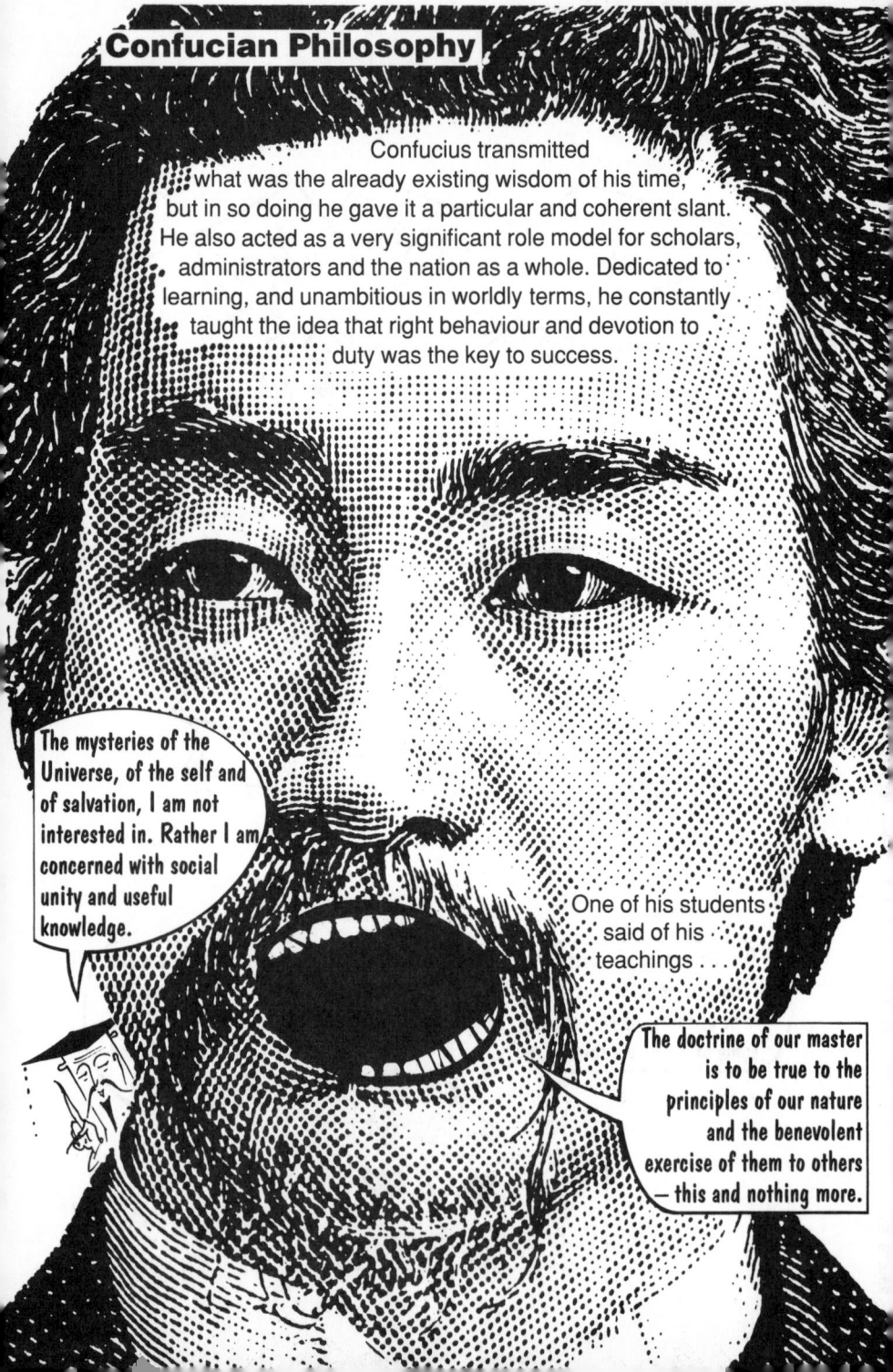
Confucian Philosophy
Confucius transmitted what was the already existing wisdom of his time, but in so doing he gave it a particular and coherent slant. He also acted as a very significant role model for scholars, administrators and the nation as a whole. Dedicated to learning, and unambitious in worldly terms, he constantly taught the idea that right behaviour and devotion to duty was the key to success.
The mysteries of the Universe, of the self and of salvation, I am not interested in. Rather I am concerned with social unity and useful knowledge.
One of his students said of his teachings . . .
The doctrine of our master is to be true to the principles of our nature and the benevolent exercise of them to others – this and nothing more.

Of learning, Confucius said . . .

If by keeping the old warm, one can provide understanding of the new, one is fit to be a teacher.

He also said . . .

If there is education there are no class-distinctions.

He took four main subjects for his teaching: conduct, culture, loyalty and good faith. Of the importance of ritual in government he said . . .

If one can govern a country by ritual and deference, there is no more to be said; but if one cannot govern a country by ritual and deference, then what has one to do with ritual?

Three Main Principles

Confucianists were concerned with the balance between individual integrity and social harmony. So there are three main principles . . .

1) **Jen**, human-heartedness (goodness, proper being).
2) **Li**, etiquette (propriety, rules).
3) **Chih**, righteousness (proper behaviour).

Negative and Positive Jen

So the way of Jen is to practise chung and shu.

How to Behave

Behaviour should be regulated by "oughtness" or what ought to be done in a particular situation. This was later described as "the principle of applying a measuring square", or working out what ought to be done by applying the rules and sticking to them.

Moral excellence, then, was expressed by the combination of right behaviour, right approach and integrity, exemplified in the person of the **Chun-Tzu** (or gentleman). Confucius himself is, of course, the ultimate model for all of these approaches and therein lies the reason for his endurance.

Mencius

Confucius' great disciple **Mencius** (371–289 B.C.) developed and codified the sage's ideas, as well as trying to explain why man should act in the right way.

The central question was precisely the nature of human nature: was it good, bad or indifferent, or all three? Mencius said there were three theories besides his own.

1) That all men are good and bad.
2) That men are neither good nor bad.
3) That some are good and some are bad.

Mencius, being a bit of an optimist, claimed that we are all born with a capacity for goodness, what he called the "four beginnings". He argued that we are all born with a sense of **Jen** (humanity), **I** (righteousness), **Li** (propriety), and **Chih** (wisdom). If these innate properties are allowed to grow normally they will develop into the four constant virtues. Just as right behaviour in human relationships is the basis of all ethics, so proper behaviour is the hallmark of a good citizen and a moral state. This is why a ruler should be a gentleman and a sage, rather like Plato's philosopher King. Indeed, if a ruler does not rule wisely and morally, the people have a right to overthrow him.
This radical idea only appeared in the West in the 17th and 18th centuries.
Mencius was bandied about in the revolutions of this century in China, particularly when he said . . .
The people are the most important element in a state, the spirits of the land and the grain are secondary, and the sovereign is the least.

For Mencius, family life was the proper way to implement Jen. For a proper state to operate, this meant the fair distribution of land, in what he called the "well-field" system. Like other aspects of Chinese philosophy, this embodied a rational, unitary and socially cohesive way of running things. It wasn't always followed, of course.

Some say that Mencius extended the teachings of Confucius on the self-cultivation of the individual outwards to the cultivation of all.

Others say that he was far too much of an idealist.

The family is the microcosm of the state.

Like Confucius, he supported **ritual**, the **family**, and the idea of the **Golden Mean**.

The School of Names

Put simply, these philosophers were interested in the meaning of names. Confucius called it the "rectification of names", by which he meant getting it right when giving something a name. (Calling a spade a spade?) In other words, the proper description and analysis of things is necessary in order to avoid falsehood and illusion. The question is of the relationship between **Ming** (the name) and **Shih** (the actuality).

They even used the example of

"What is a table?"

made famous by Bertrand Russell, rather later on.

The Problem of Universals

The debates within the **School of Names** were sometimes just complex and tricky interpretations of the way things mean (**sophistry**, it came to be called by the Greeks). The important philosophical point to it all was the nature of **universals**, or how language describes things.

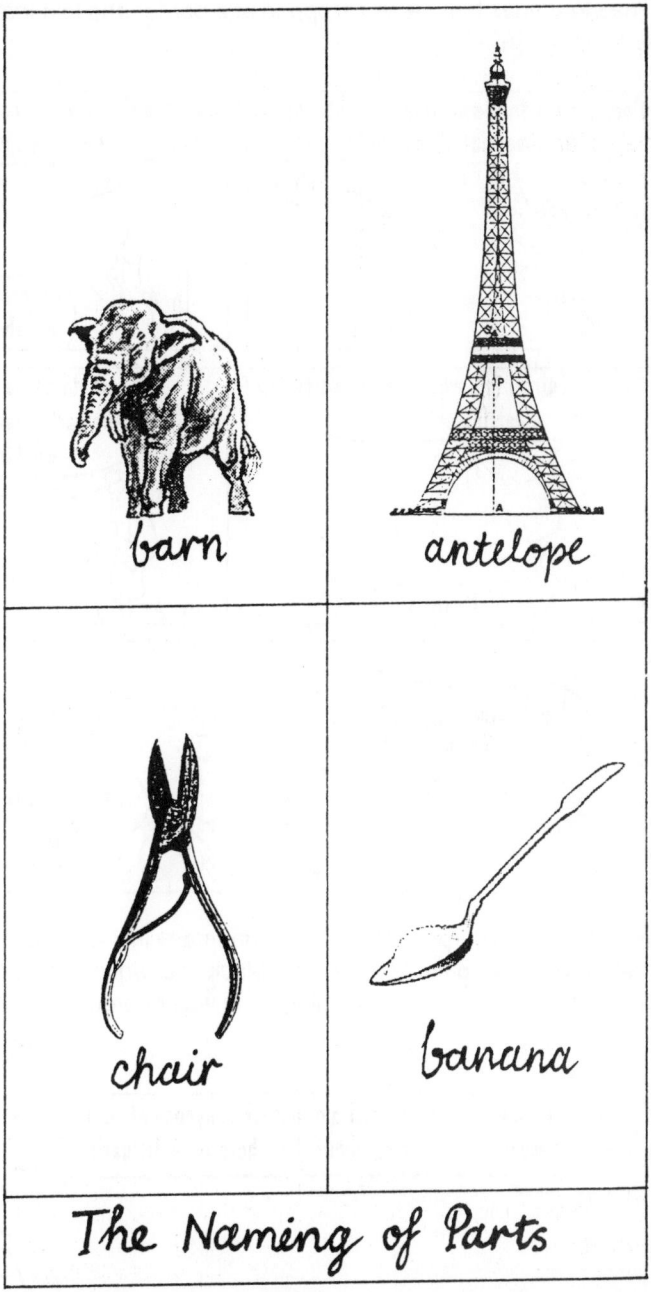

One of the more famous members of the Names school was **Kung-sun Lung** (4th century B.C.), who wrote the famous "White Horse Discourse". The story goes that he was stopped at a border and told that horses were not allowed in.

It comes as no surprise to discover that many in the School of Names were lawyers who could argue that black was white. Confucius himself had a healthy dislike of legal things and was quoted as saying . . .

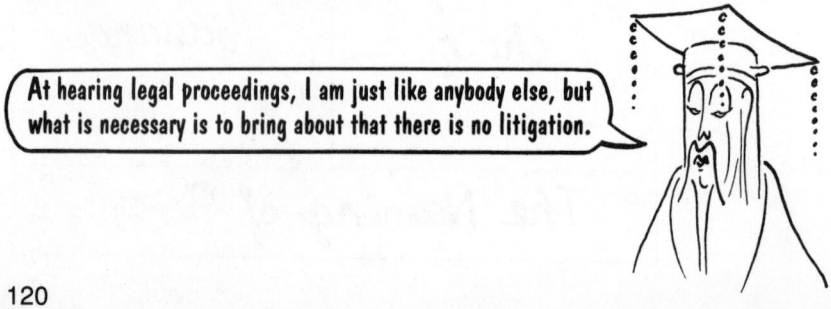

The Mohist School

Based on the work of **Mo-Tzu** (c. 479–381 B.C.), and on the book of the same name, this school was anti-Confucian and anti-tradition. Mo criticized Confucius' love of ritual and music from the standpoint of the lower classes, who were excluded from such noble goings on. It is said that Mo-Tzu represented the class of knights (**Hseih**) who did the fighting rather than the talking, and were therefore rather more practical about institutions and rituals.

The **Mohist** school had a practical and utilitarian approach, but it did speak of an all-embracing love which was meant to be the guiding principle of all action.

Anti-Confucius

Mo-Tzu said that Confucius got it all wrong on four major counts.
1) The Confucianists did not believe in spirits or gods, which would displease them.
2) The Confucianists believed that one should mourn parents for three years, which wasted everybody's time and energy.
3) They liked music which also wasted everybody's time.
4) Confucianists seemed to believe in a predetermined fate, which made everybody passive and lazy.

Mo-Tzu also didn't think much of all the learning and ritual that Confucianists went in for.

His was a practical, all-embracing, hearty sort of "let's all get on with it" philosophy.

Mohist Dialectics

The Mohists' utilitarian view of the world led them to defend commonsense and to dismiss most philosophical speculation. They disliked the Taoists in particular for their other-worldliness and their disdain for practical knowledge.

Their idea of all-embracing love sounds very nice, but how are you supposed to love everybody?

Even the person who robs you?

Oddly enough, the Mohists were very keen on the **dialectic** as a means of reasoning and rebutting their opponents' arguments. It seems odd because the dialectic (thesis-antithesis-synthesis) is often associated in philosophy with difficult, obscure and theoretical approaches to the world. So we can say the Mohists provided quite a complex way of arguing for straightforward commonsense and utilitarian approaches.

Of the benefits, choose the greatest. Of the harms, choose the slightest.

The Fa Chia, or Legalist School

Whereas Confucius argued that good government was based on tradition, ritual and loyalty, the **Legalist School**, as its name suggests, argued for the rule of law. They did not believe, like many of the other philosophers, that a natural moral law would take care of how people should behave, but rather that a fixed code of law had to be drawn up and enforced. **Han-Tzu** (280–233 B.C.) was one of the reformers who belonged to this school of modernizers.

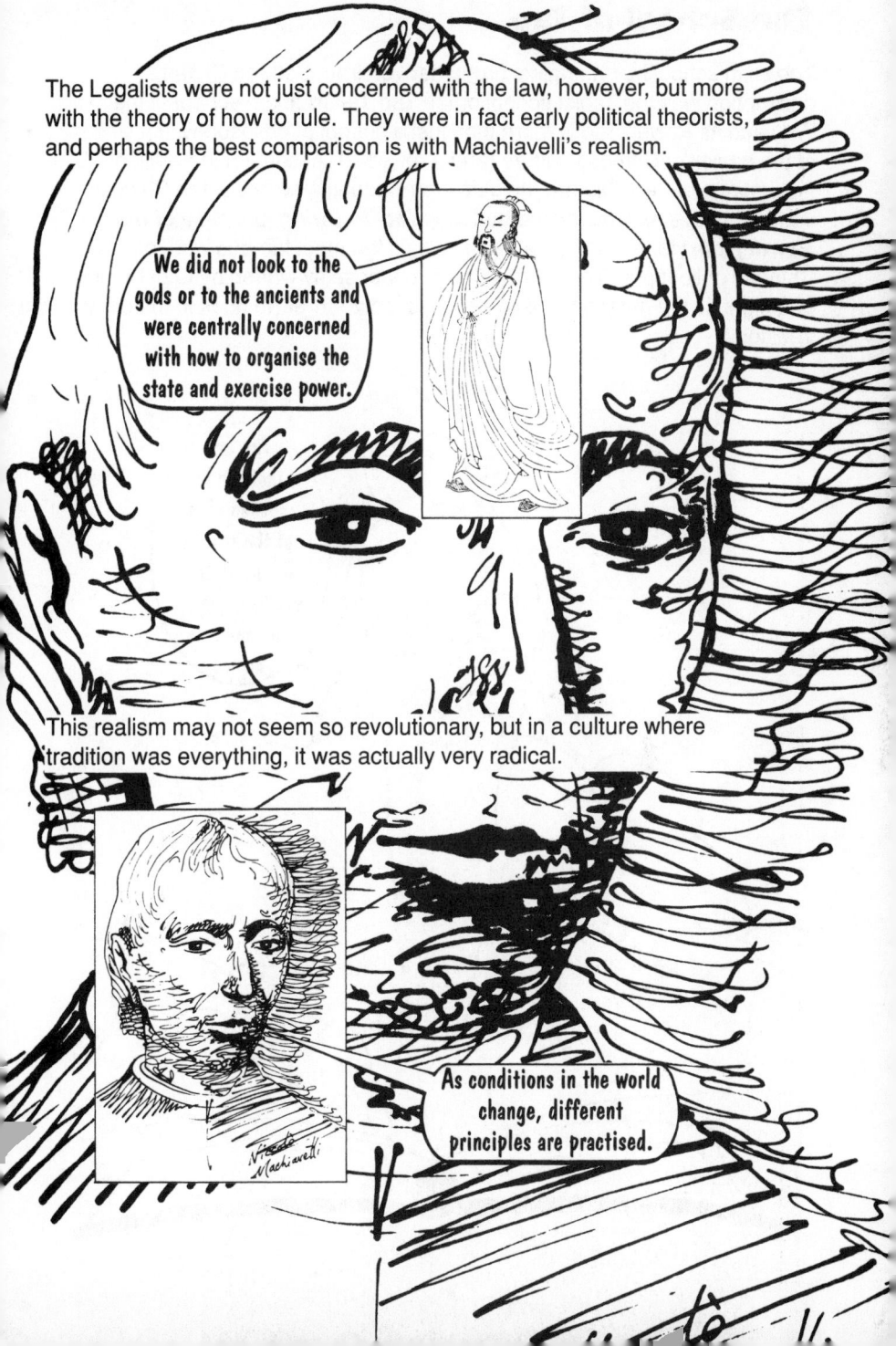
The Legalists were not just concerned with the law, however, but more with the theory of how to rule. They were in fact early political theorists, and perhaps the best comparison is with Machiavelli's realism.
We did not look to the gods or to the ancients and were centrally concerned with how to organise the state and exercise power.
This realism may not seem so revolutionary, but in a culture where tradition was everything, it was actually very radical.
Niccolò Machiavelli
As conditions in the world change, different principles are practised.

The School of Tao

The sixth school in the original group derived from Ssu-ma Ch'ien's description was the Taoist school or the **Tao Te-Chia**, the school of the Way and its Power. Tao is more than just a school of philosophy. It is one of the basics of Chinese culture (and a religion!). According to tradition, the writings of **Lao-Tzu** are the oldest philosophical works of the Chinese canon, but this may be inaccurate. The ***Tao Te Ching*** (the ***Way of the Power***), next to the Confucian *Analects*, is the most famous work of Chinese philosophy. The *Tao Te Ching*, supposedly written by Lao-Tzu in one night, is the most aphoristic and least down-to-earth book in the early tradition.

The Way

Tao actually means the "Way" or the Universal Path. It is the force that governs the Universe. Or as the *Tao Te Ching* puts it:

The Tao gives birth to the One;
The One gives birth to the Two;
The Two gives birth to the Three;
The Three gives birth to all things.

This is clearly a much more abstract approach than many of the other schools. The central idea of Tao is a terribly slippery one, over which there is rather a lot of debate. To see Tao as a force, a power (**Te** means power) and a way of relating to it is perhaps the clearest approximation.

Only through relating to the power of Tao, in harmony with the forces of nature, can one's Te be achieved.

Wu-Wei

Liu Hsin said that the Taoists came from the hermits. Confucius said they were **Yin Che**, "those who obscure themselves". . .

Because of their position on the forces of nature and the ultimately unchanging reality that lay behind all change, the Taoists generally wanted to escape from the world, not interfere with it. Lao-Tzu tells us . . .

This principle of "letting be" they called **Wu-Wei**.

The Power of Te

Confucianists said that the Taoists were just selfish, or "each one for himself". One of the early Taoists, **Yang Chu**, is supposed to have said that he wouldn't have exchanged ruling the world for one hair off his back, which seems a little bit extreme. Their basic argument is that one should despise things and value life, which seems more reasonable.
As Yang Chu put it . . .

Taoists aimed at a life of simplicity and harmony with Tao, not being ruled by intellect, but by a natural power, or Te.

To preserve self, Taoists argued, the proper way was to regulate one's behaviour according to the underlying rules of nature. Lao-Tzu summed it all up.

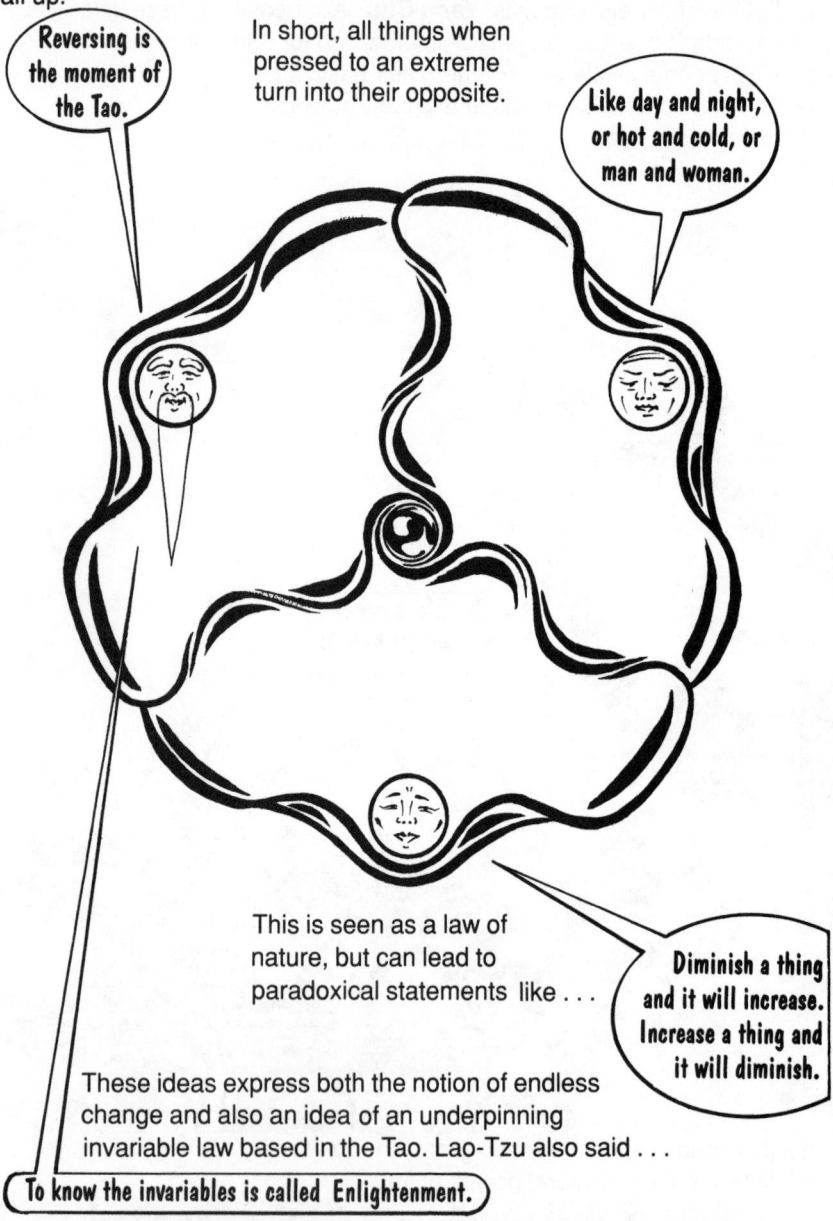

So true knowledge is knowing the basis of all things, the way of the Tao.

One of the main themes of Taoism is the notion of Wu-Wei, or "non- action".

To follow the way of the Tao, to exercise the power of the Tao (the Te) is to practise Wu-Wei.

Tao and Politics

Did Lao-Tzu exist and live in the sixth century B.C.? Did he write the book bearing his name in the one night before he "went West"? We have to exercise Wu-Wei here and just look at the book of the name and accept its existence without questioning the history too much. As Lao-Tzu said . . .

Lao-Tzu's political theory was based on this premise as well.

Chuang-Tzu

After Lao-Tzu (which also means Old Master), there were others who developed Taoist philosophy. **Chuang-Tzu** (369–286 B.C.) was another great exponent of Taoism and reputedly lived as a hermit.

The text that bears his name, the ***Chuang-Tzu***, undoubtedly written much later by his disciples, tells us this sort of thing. Chuang-Tzu was all for living according to nature, avoiding artificiality and government of any sort, and following the way of the Tao as the unity of opposites. He was apparently very famous in his own time and turned down any offers of running things.

Nature and Knowledge

Taoism might be seen as just accepting the way the world is, living by its rules and trying to avoid any difficulties. A Confucian cynic might say that the fantastic allegories and paradoxical sayings of the Taoists didn't add up to anything other than the avoidance of complex realities. Take Chuang-Tzu's argument about the nature of different abilities in things. He says . . .

Actually, Chuang-Tzu is making an important point that nature and knowledge are specific to specific things, and happiness comes from being true to your proper nature, or Te.

Happiness of the Sage

The Taoists were very interested in ways of achieving absolute happiness, of harmony with one's Te, or innate nature. For example, there is discussion in the *Chuang-Tzu* on death, on the fear and anxiety that accompany it.

So the ultimate Tao sage is one who has transcended emotion, worldly attachments and distractions and is at one with the Tao, the nameless and the nothingness.

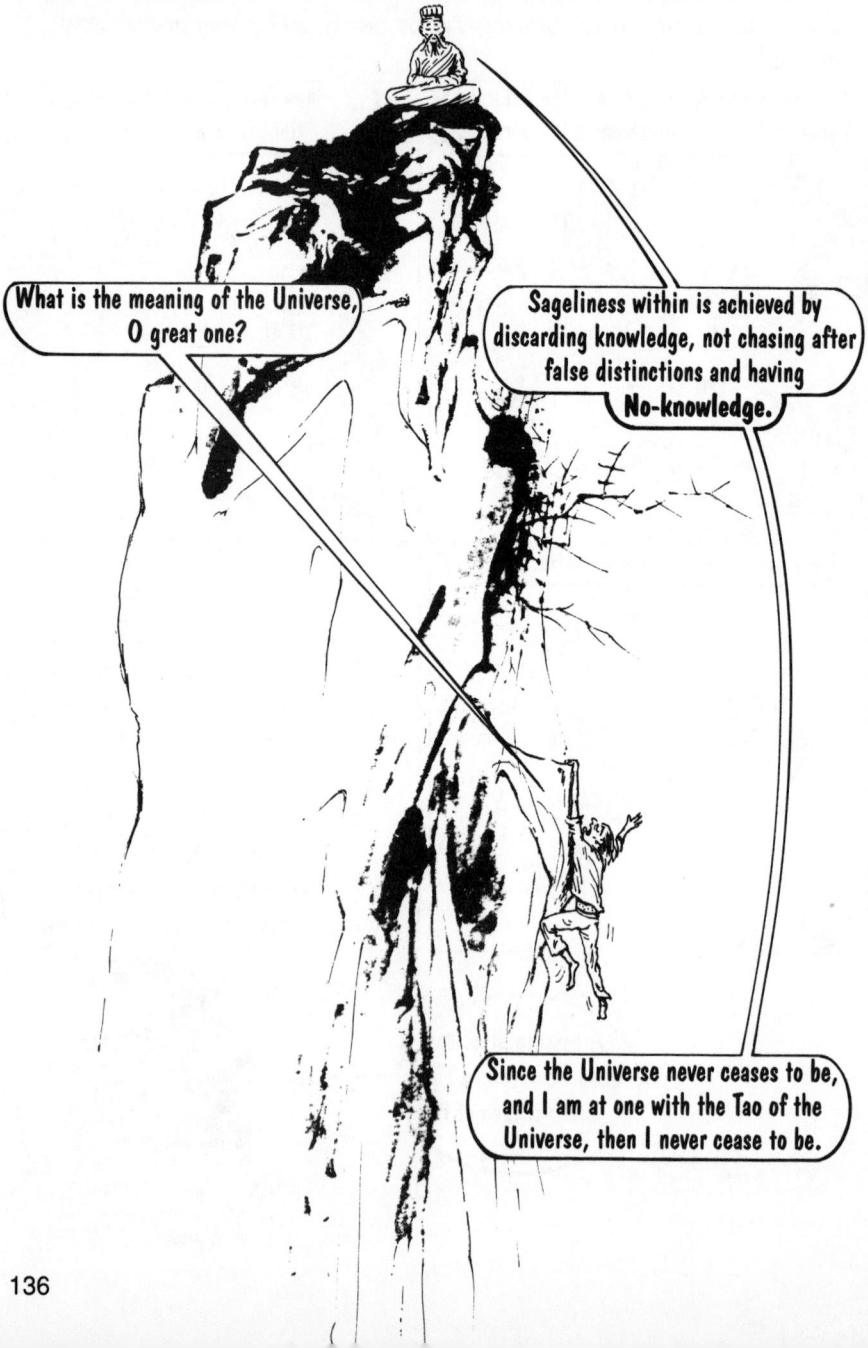

By the time of the two historians, Ssu-ma Ch'ien (died 110 B.C) and Liu Hsin (46 B.C.–A.D. 23), there was an increasing eclecticism within Chinese philosophy. Different kinds of approaches were lifted from each school. The ***Great Appendix to the Yi*** (the ***Yi Wen Chih*** or "Treatise on Literature" derived from Liu Hsin), puts it like this . . .

This very much represents the eclectic spirit of Chinese philosophy. Despite their dismissal of each other, Confucianism and Taoism share that general approach of "Sageliness within and Kingliness without".

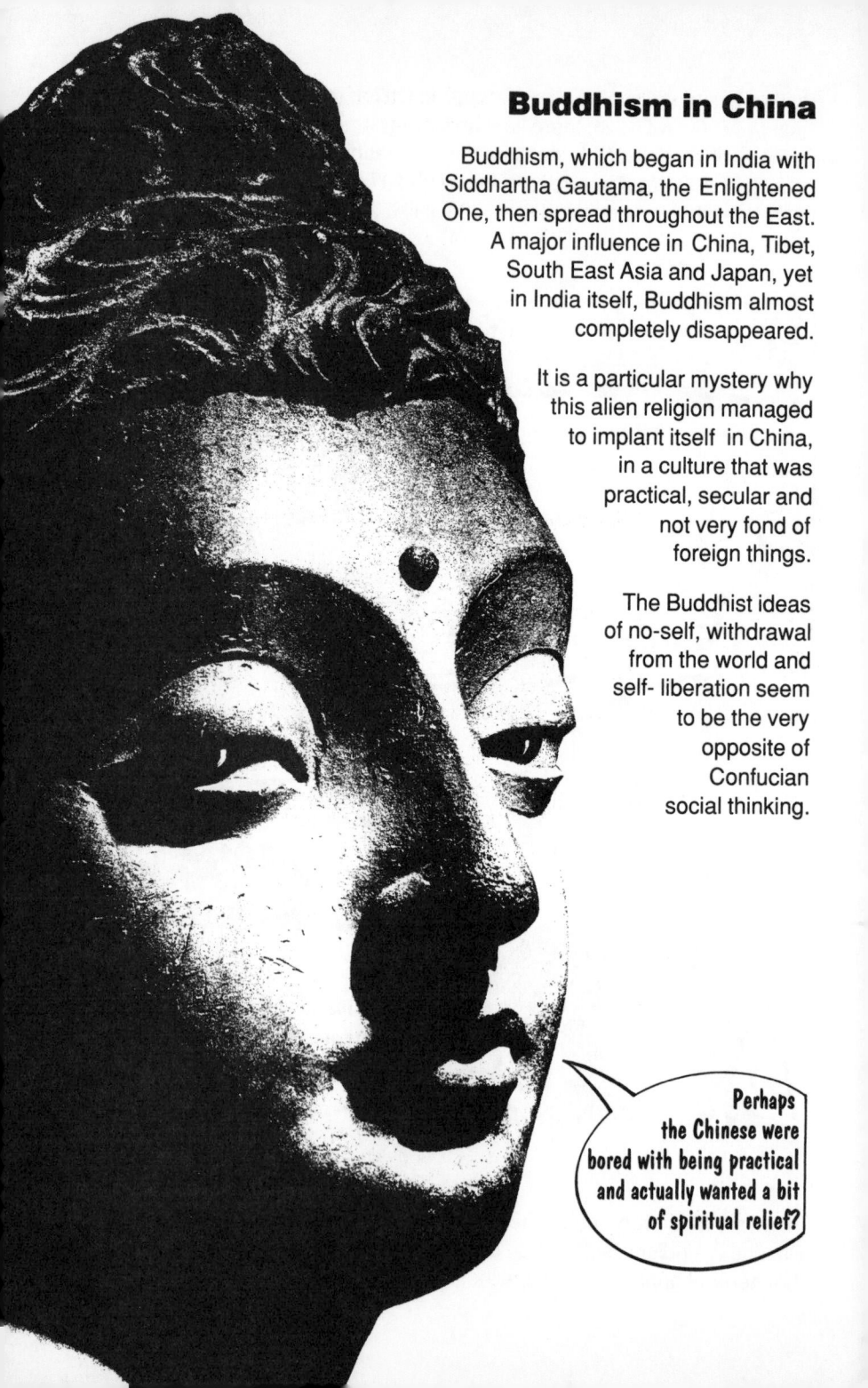

Buddhism in China

Buddhism, which began in India with Siddhartha Gautama, the Enlightened One, then spread throughout the East. A major influence in China, Tibet, South East Asia and Japan, yet in India itself, Buddhism almost completely disappeared.

It is a particular mystery why this alien religion managed to implant itself in China, in a culture that was practical, secular and not very fond of foreign things.

The Buddhist ideas of no-self, withdrawal from the world and self- liberation seem to be the very opposite of Confucian social thinking.

How Buddhism Arrived in China

Buddhist ideas probably filtered into China via the silk route and the channels of trade, but the opposition to them was official, cultural and powerful. Perhaps because the officials championed Confucianism and Taoism, the people took to the Buddhist message of liberation.

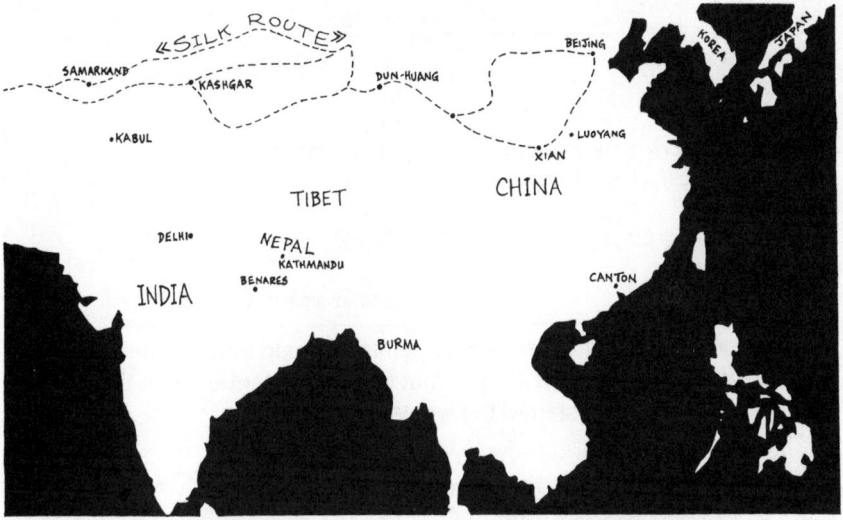

The condition of the Chinese peasantry was seriously grim.

Something that promised definite release would seem attractive.

Whatever the reasons, the introduction of Buddhism to China was a "cultural revolution" with a long-term impact.

The other-worldliness of Taoism may also explain the reception of Buddhism. Both have in common a search for universal Enlightenment and a rejection of worldly ties.

Different versions of Buddhism had developed in India, particularly the **Hinayana** (small vehicle) and **Mahayana** (great vehicle). So, in China too, we find different schools: the two most influential were **Ch'an** (Zen) and the **Middle Path**. The others were:

Chinese Buddhist Schools	
School	*Prominent Figure*
Three Treatises (San-lun) or Middle Doctrine	Chi-tsang (549–623)
Consciousness Only or Mere Ideation	Hsüan-tsang (596–664)
T'ien-T'ai (Fa-hua) or Lotus School	Chih-k'ai (538–597)
Hua-yen or Wreath School	Fa-tsang (643–712)
Ch'an	Bodhidharma (fl. 460–534)

Taoists and Confucianists, at various points, claimed that Buddhism really started in China. One story is that Lao-Tzu, after he "went West", taught the Buddha and started the whole thing.

"Going West" is a polite way of saying "kicking the bucket".

Indian Missionaries

In fact, Buddhism was brought to China by various Indian missionaries. Chinese scholars who visited India also brought back ideas and texts which were then translated. It is thought that the influence of Buddhism began during the reign of **Emperor Ming** (A.D. 58–75), but was seen as rather occultish. During the third and fourth centuries, more and more Buddhist texts were translated and their influence grew, possibly as a result of the political turmoil of the times. **Kumarajiva** (343–413), who introduced the ***Madhyamika Sastra***, was so influential that he was held captive at the court and developed his ideas whilst translating texts.

Ch'an Buddhism

Bodhidharma (460–534) brought in Ch'an (Zen) which later became important in Japan. Ch'an emphasized meditation and study.

It is anti-philosophical by not relying on words or conceptual understanding. They studied **Koans**, which are like little riddles, to point you at the nature of ultimate reality.

Karma or Yeh

The idea of karma, translated into Chinese as **Yeh**, is still central in Chinese Buddhism, as is the idea that the individual is responsible for actions that produce consequences.

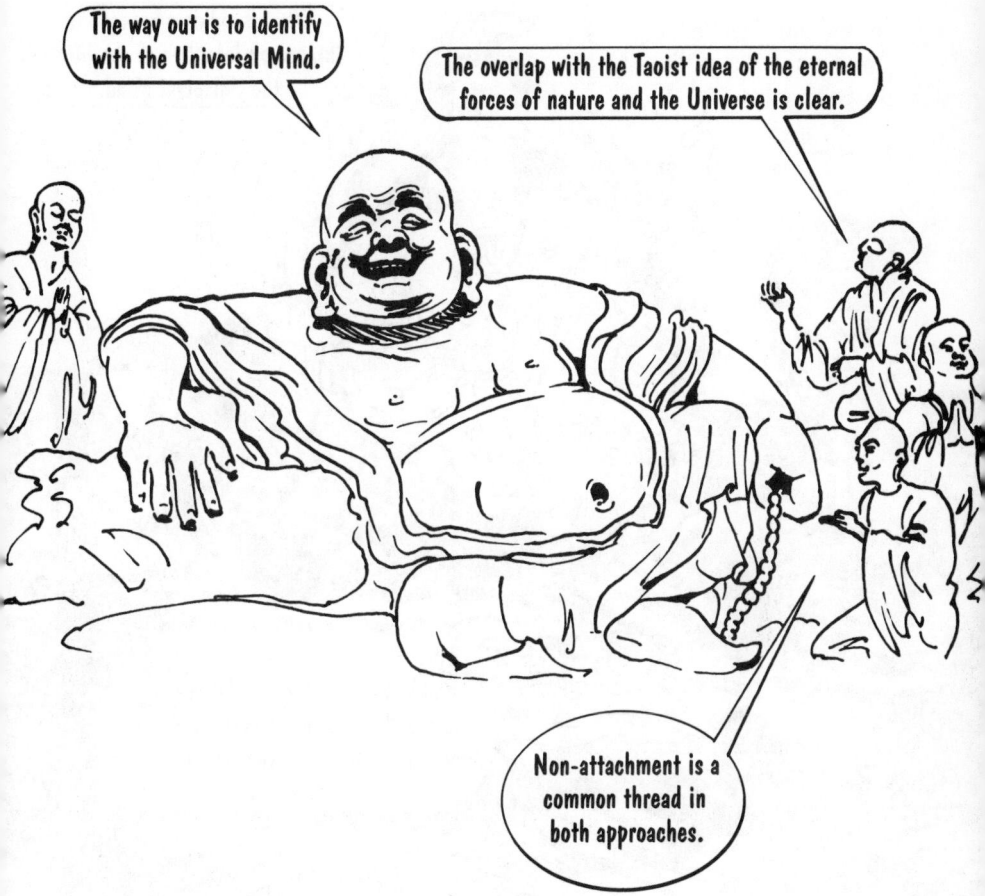

The Mahayana school of Buddhism believes in showing compassion to all things and people. Its more egalitarian approach perhaps explains why it took off in repressive Chinese society.

The ignorance which leads the mind to seek the world, which is illusory, is called **Wu-Ming**, from the Sanskrit, **Avidya**. The aim is to achieve nirvana or Enlightenment. Nirvana is similar to the Taoist notion of no-self blending with the forces of the Universe. But it also means clicking in with the **Universal Mind**.

Japanese Buddhism

The introduction of Buddhism to Japan in the 6th century A.D. was the crucial step in the development of Japanese philosophy. This led eventually to the formation of the Japanese form of **Zen** Buddhism, which epitomizes the special character of the Japanese Way.

There are many other philosophies in Japanese history, but none which better conveys the essence of Japanese thought than Zen.

What is Zen?

Zen is unique and puts the uninitiated out of their wits.
One master, when asked the nature of Zen, said . . .
I raise my eyebrows, I move my eyes.
He meant that the nature of Zen is both ordinary and extraordinary and can be conveyed in almost anything.
Zen is the attempt to fathom the mysterious nature of things and beings.
Zen is the art of living Zen.
It also permeates the Samurai Warrior code of **Bushido.**

Key Zen Ideas

The many different forms of Buddhism all seek after Enlightenment, the fundamental idea of no-self and liberation from the world. Debates about what constitutes nirvana are irrelevant to the Ch'an (Zen) school's answer that it is inexpressible.

Zen took over from Ch'an certain key ideas, but Zen thought is a long way from original Buddhist principles.

Its key ideas are . . .
1) Genuine Enlightenment is **instantaneous**. Preparation may be necessary, but true realization is a total experience.

2) Zen involves action through non-action, working towards a result in which no-self is exercised.

3) Enlightenment and ordinary experience are related, but scriptures, texts and theory do not provide the path to nirvana.

4) A true sage lives in every man and in all things. One does not have to retreat to the mountains to find Enlightenment.

Is Zen a Philosophy?

If philosophy in its broadest sense is understanding the world we live in, then Zen philosophy is clearly that. In terms of Western logic, however, it isn't "properly" philosophy. Japanese ways of thinking about the world are concerned with the clarity and precision of images, rather than with formal logic. Japanese philosophy can be seen in its art, its calligraphy, its ritual, in the order and interconnectedness of its culture. This is its secret.

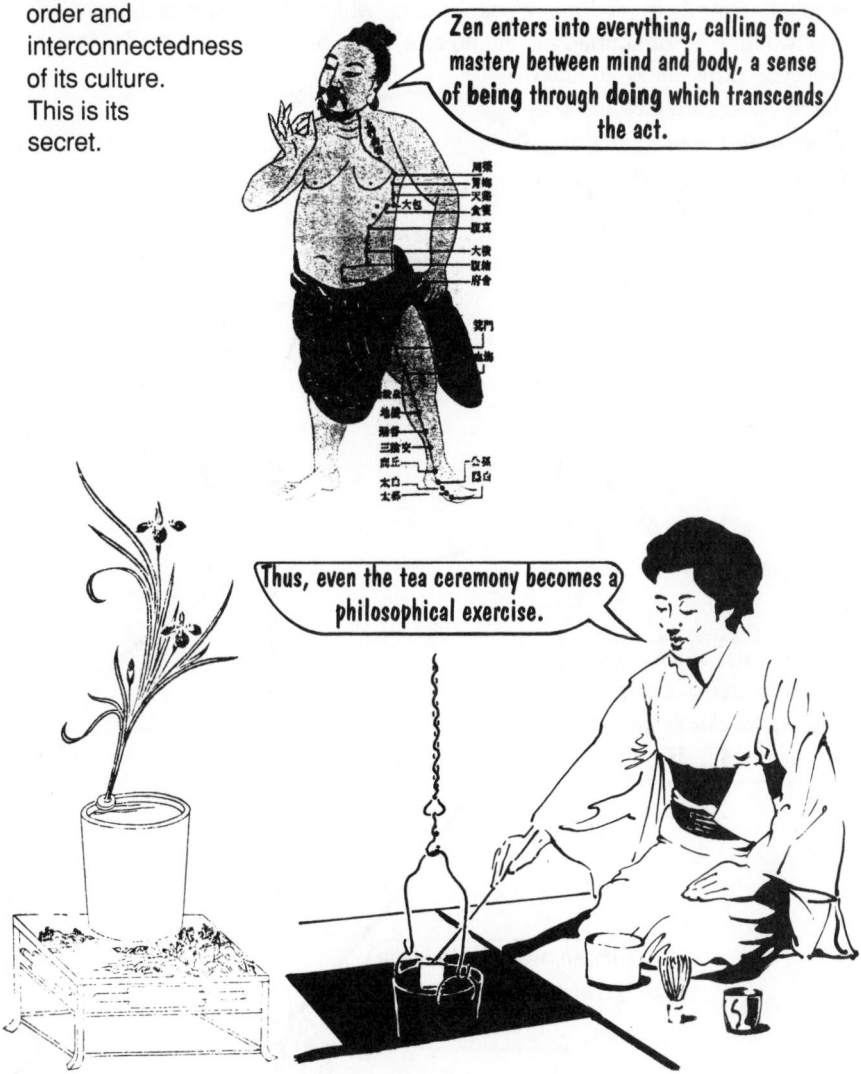

Dogen, Zen Master

The most famous exponent of Zen in Japan is **Dogen** (1200–53). His work ***Shobogenzo*** (***Treasury of the True Dharma Eye***) is the first Buddhist text written in Japanese, rather than classical Chinese. It is said to be the first truly philosophical work in Japan and is certainly difficult. Dogen strongly urged meditation. The word Zen ultimately derives from the Sanskrit for meditation, which Dogen called **Zazen** (seated meditation).

Meditation leads to the intuitive experience which transcends ordinary reality. It can be described as finding one's true nature. One aims for the losing of "body-mind" to achieve a non-conceptual awareness. The impermanence of the world is emphasized by Dogen.

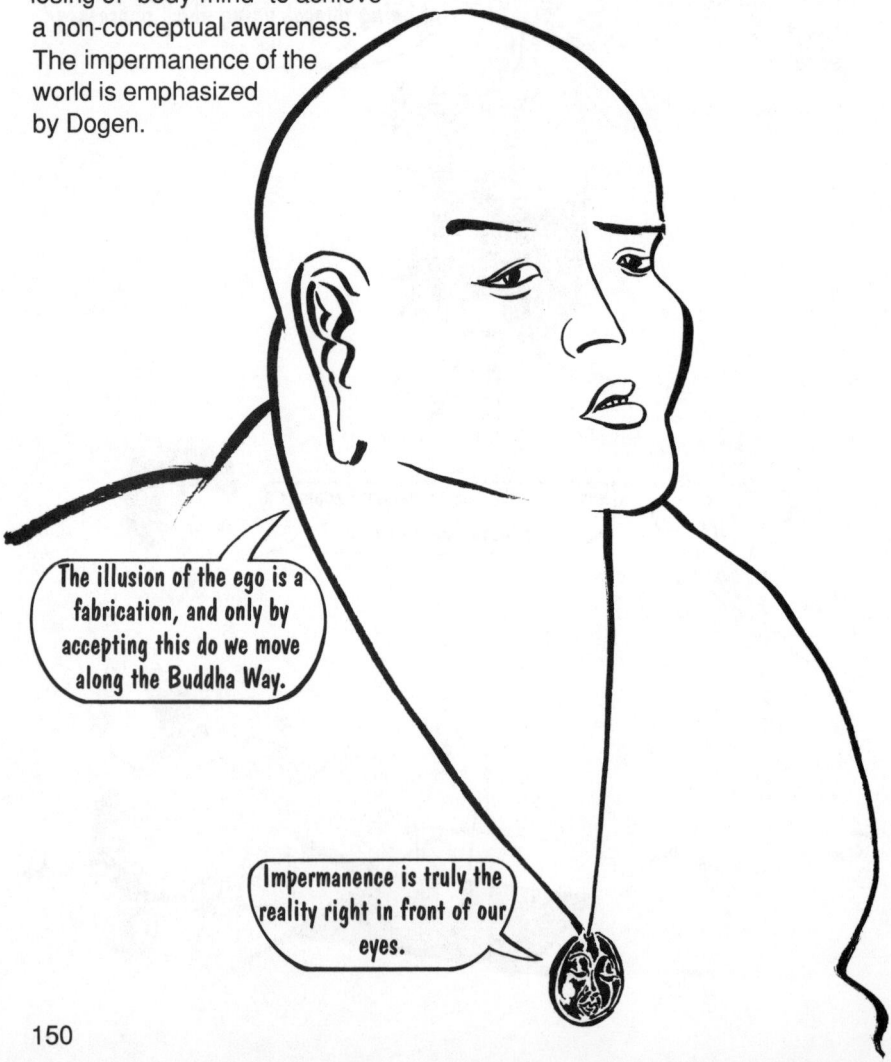

Dogen also emphasizes the Buddha-nature or enlightened nature of the whole world.

Buddha-nature is that "nothingness" that we must recognize as the essential emptiness of all things. Things do not have a meaning in themselves, but only in relation to other things.

For Westerners obsessed with the classification of material things, this is a truly radical idea. Dogen goes on to say . . .

Buddha-nature is vast emptiness, open, clear and bright.

The impermanence of things also led Dogen to speculate about the nature of Time itself. The past, the present and the future are combined in the moments of Enlightenment.

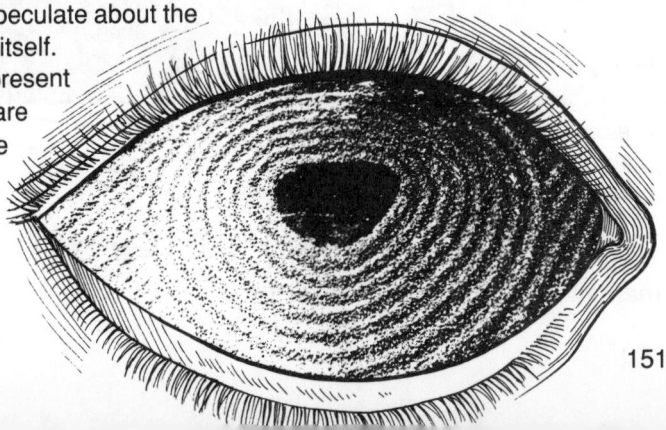

Neo-Confucianism in China

After a long period of wars and civil disarray, China was reunited in 589 under the **Sui** dynasty, and with this came a revival of Confucianism. For some time, the Confucianists had attacked the Buddhists for their escapism and anti-social attitudes. The restored Imperial Court also sought to restore Confucianism to its central role in Chinese cultural life.

The underlying pattern of Chinese culture, based on family, agriculture and social relations, simply reasserted itself.

Under the **Tang** dynasty (618–906), a centralized and powerful court ruled supreme once again, and a pair of brothers, both philosophers, emerged to rethink Confucianism. **Han Yu** (768–824) and **Li Ao** (died 844) set about putting the philosophical house in order. Li Ao, in an essay ***On the Restoration of Nature***, summed up the superior Confucian approach.

Ch'i, The Great Harmony

The philosopher **Chang Tsai** (1020–77) emphasized the importance of **Ch'i** in his ***Cheng Meng***, or

Ch'i originally meant simply gas or ether, but with the Neo-Confucianists became a much more abstract and difficult idea. Chang Tsai describes Ch'i as being the basic matter of the Universe, rather like the way Plato conceived of matter.

Plato

I took it further and said Ch'i was the physical matter that makes up all things.

Ch'i is described as the Great Harmony or the Supreme Ultimate in his *Beginners* book.

The Great Harmony is known as the Tao.

Ch'i and Social Morality

Although it may not seem obvious, Chang Tsai was trying to get away from Taoist and Buddhist ideas of non-being, and back to a position where social morality was important. If everything was simply nothingness, then it was difficult to argue for social ethics. Nihilism could be just as sensible. Therefore he said . . .

He argued that the Void was not an absolute vacuum, that the Ch'i was dispersed in a way that was not visible.

Chang Tsai therefore gave back to Confucianism a philosophical basis for social morality, which was an important thing to do.

One very famous passage from the *Cheng Meng* became known as the "Western Inscription", because Chang Tsai had it up on the Western wall of his study:

Neo-Confucianists were fond of this because it clearly distinguished the Confucian approach from the Buddhist and Taoist.

The Form of Li

The nature of **Li** and **Ch'i** is very similar to the Western philosophical debate about the form and matter of things found in Plato and Aristotle.

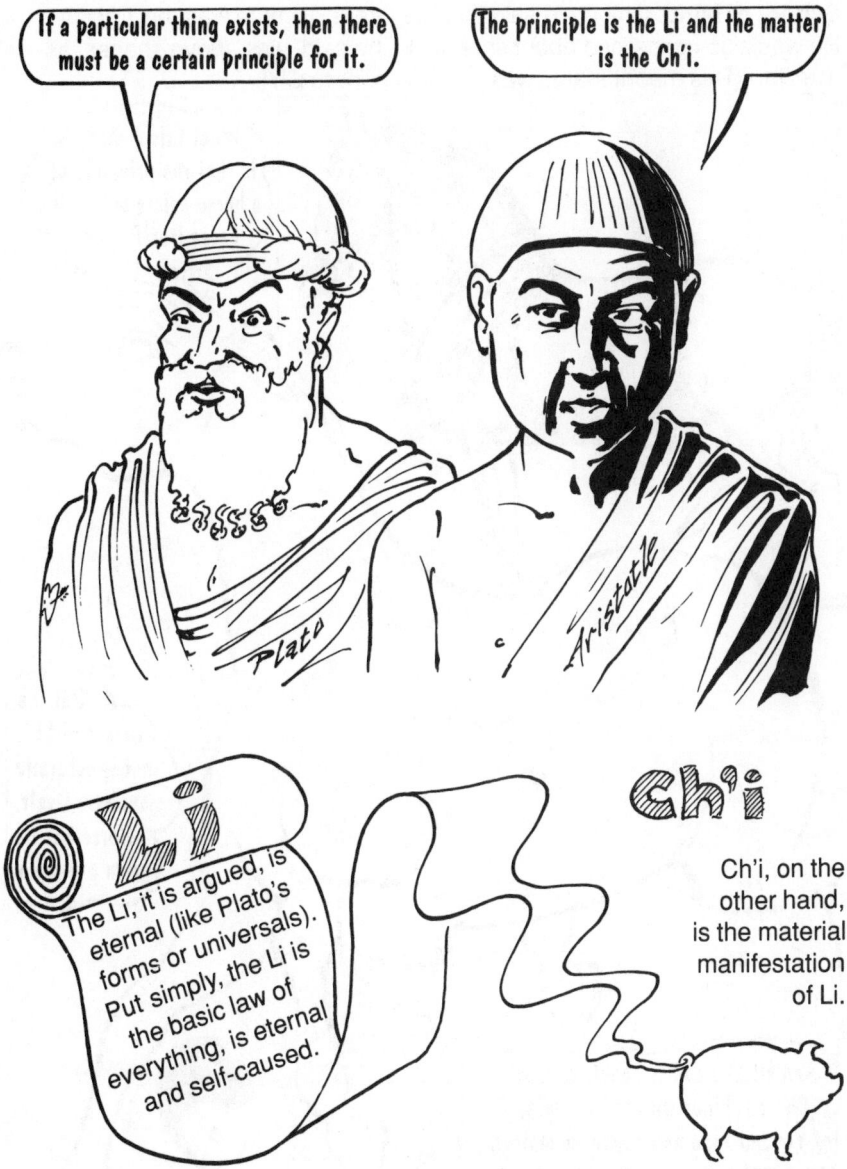

The Two Schools

Brothers seemed to play quite an important role in Neo-Confucianism. Another pair, known as the Ch'eng Masters, started what became known as the Two Schools. **Ch'eng Yi** (1033–1108) inaugurated the **School of Laws or Principles** and his big brother **Ch'eng Hao** (1032–1085) the **School of Mind**. Ch'eng Yi said that the Great Ultimate was the T'ai Chi. He was also concerned about shapes. Li, he said, was above shapes, as was Tao. This meant that Li was logically prior to Ch'i.

Chu-Tzu

The School of Laws was completed by Chu-Hsi, also known as **Chu-Tzu** (1130–1200), called the St. Thomas Aquinas of China. This means he produced a complete metaphysical system of philosophy that was rather scholastic. His recorded sayings run to about 140 books, besides commentaries on the famous ***Four Books*** which became the main texts used in state examinations.

The four books were

Chu-Tzu synthesized the basic doctrines of the Confucian philosophers into a coherent unity and clarified the Li and Ch'i debate. "For everything there is a Li, which makes it what it ought to be, or a thing is a concrete instance of its Li." At the same time, there must be an ultimate standard for the whole Universe, which embraces all Li. This is called the Supreme Ultimate or the T'ai Chi. (We in the West usually put God in here to explain things.)

When called upon to explain the connection between the Supreme Ultimate, the Li and the Ch'i, Chu-Tzu used a metaphor about the moon.

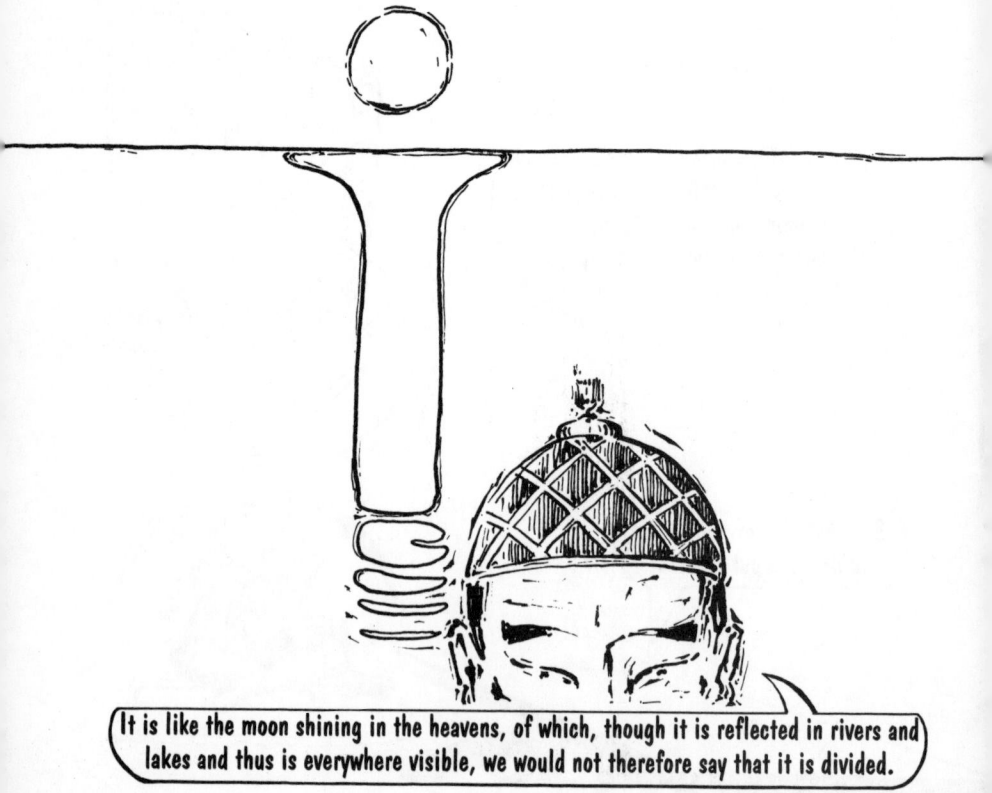

Neo-Confucian Politics

In terms of politics, Chu-Tzu proposed all of the Confucian values – a philosopher-sage as ruler and a people who lived a life of virtue. Man, he argued, had the Great Ultimate within him. It was a matter of bringing it out through self-cultivation and the investigation of things. Again, Chu-Tzu sounds like Plato, with a collective approach much like Plato's Republic in which wisdom and order are put above individuality and self-expression.

The School of Mind

The School of Mind begun by Ch'eng Hao was completed by **Lu Chu-Yuan** (1139–93) and **Wang Shou-Jen** (1472–1529). Lu Chu-Yuan is supposed to have had a sudden enlightenment and said . . .

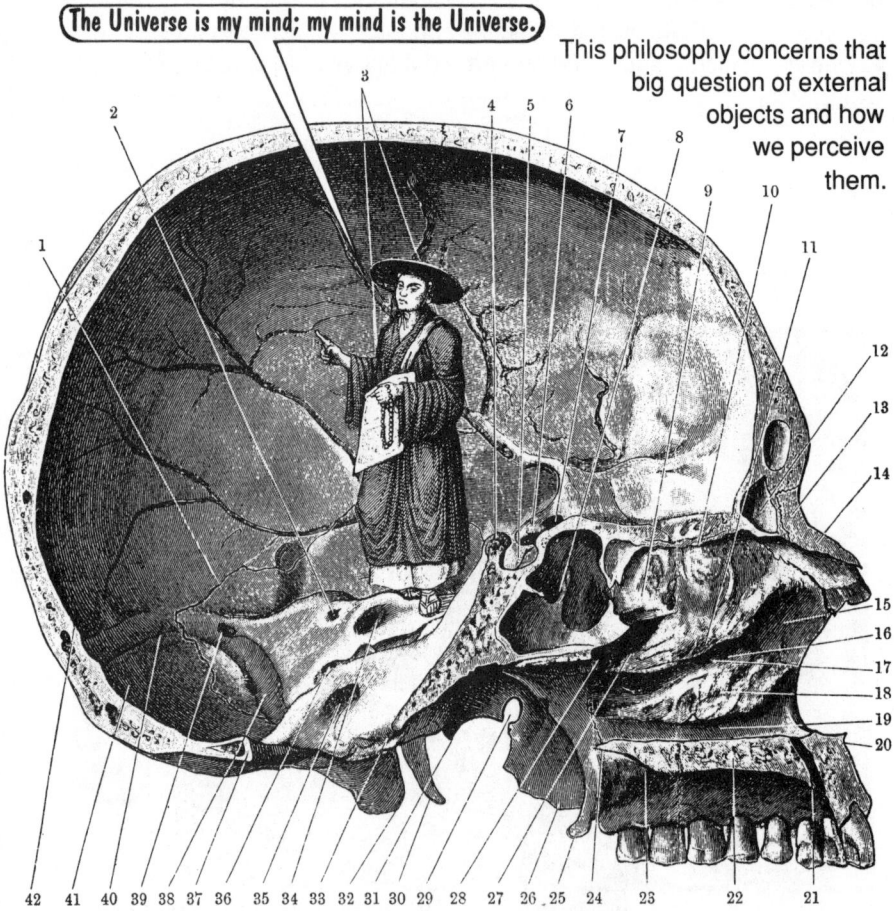

This philosophy concerns that big question of external objects and how we perceive them.

This philosophical argument was clearly going to run and run, just as it did in the West.

Wang Shou-Jen's argument for intuitive knowledge was based on the Unity of Thought and Action. He criticized the Taoists and the Buddhists for their escapism and their refusal to think about practical human relations. He stressed that very Chinese, and Eastern, idea of the unity and interconnectedness of all things.

He was followed by the **Empirical School** which also advocated a return to Confucius and Mencius. **Tai Chen** (1723–77) was the greatest exponent of this approach, which sought to re-establish a more practical philosophy.

Modern China

At the turn of this century, in 1898, there was a reform movement in China against the inept **Manchu** governments and the dire influence of Europe.

Reform meant going back to the classics.

One leading philosopher, **K'ang Yu-Wei** (1858–1927), argued the case that Confucius had really been a reformer, not a conservative.

This could be shown in his philosophy.

The "Hundred Days of Reform" got off to a good start but rapidly ran out of steam. Many people, including the philosopher **T'an Ssu-Tung** (1837–1909), were executed.

I had attempted to synthesize the Mencian idea of love with modern physics and chemistry. My quest for the new age of Great Unity cost me my head.

Influences from the West were few and far between, but the American pragmatist philosopher, **John Dewey** (1859–1952) and the British logician, **Bertrand Russell** (1872–1970) went to Peking in 1919–20 to deliver lectures at the University. There is not much sign that they radically altered traditional Chinese philosophy.

What the Chinese made of Dewey's pragmatic notion of truth and Bertrand Russell's rampant individualism is anybody's guess.

Yen-Fu (1853–1920) was the greatest authority on Western thought at the turn of the century, and translated a number of Western classics.

Strangely, he recommended the British sociologist **Herbert Spencer** (1820–1903) as the greatest Western philosopher of all time. Spencer certainly was an influential social philosopher in his time, and this suggests that Yen-Fu was attracted to him because of Chinese practical concerns with social reform. Western philosophy was naturally read through the grid of Eastern philosophy.

Marxist Maoism

Marxism was the most potent form of Western thinking in China, and inspired social reform, particularly in the 1930s and 1940s, which led to the Great Revolution. But a peculiarly Chinese version of Marxism came to be officially embraced, that of **Maoism**. If you look carefully, you can see that Maoism is actually an eclectic 20th century version of Neo-Confucianism.

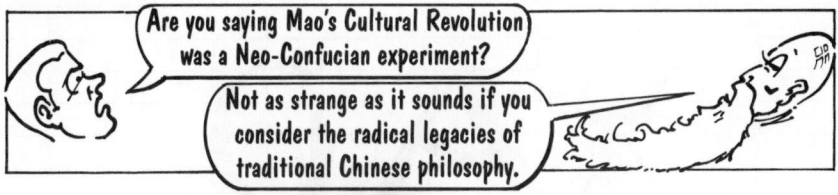

On Contradiction

Mao Tse-Tung (1893–1976) put himself forward as a philosopher and justified his policies by reference to dialectical thinking. His famous essay ***On Contradiction*** (1937) appears to be a classic statement of Marxism-Leninism-Maoism, but it echoes classical Chinese philosophy in interesting ways.

Mao's view of a hierarchy of contradictions, interpenetrating one another, sounds remarkably like the ideas of the complementarity of Yin and Yang.

Maoism is the way of social reform which Chinese radicals chose to come to terms with the West and integrate modernization into Chinese thought. Mao insisted that one had to deal with the particular and the concrete in thought, not just with theoretical abstractions. His emphasis on real historical conditions and the importance of practice, not theory, sounds very materialist but can also be understood as a form of Zen in reverse.

Mao says...

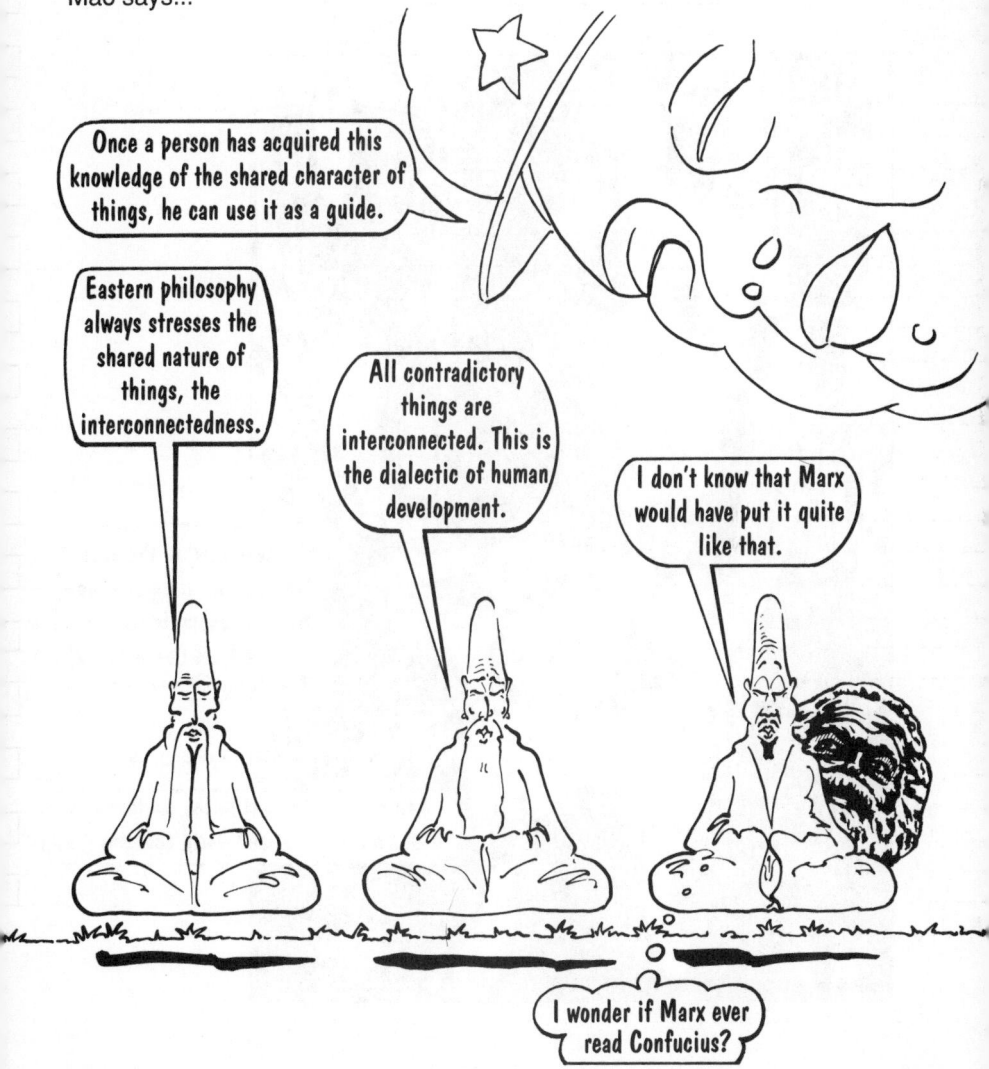

Ancient or Postmodern?

Chinese philosophy seemed to be old when it started. Confucius was always referring to traditions that went back centuries, and upholding them as examples to be followed. Some 2,500 years later, many of the same themes are present.

The late 20th century is characterized by the information superhighway and a global free market economy. The world has never seemed so homogeneous, with all of its societies mutually influenced by the same economic and cultural patterns.

Western philosophy, science and technology have been crucial in installing a universal "mass media" order, but this does not settle the question of whether Western or Eastern cultures are better equipped to grapple with "hyperreality".

Beyond East and West?

Postmodernity has also provoked a fundamentalist reaction in the East, with the threat to traditional cultures being met by "hyper"-traditionalism. Yet, we have seen how Eastern attitudes of reverence for continuity and cosmic unity are perfectly compatible with acceptance of impermanence, illusion and liberation from the ego falsehood. Eastern thinking has found ways of overcoming the apparent contradiction between change and sameness, and this may be its remedial contribution to moderating the intellectual arrogance and destructive short-sightedness of Western cultures.

Postscript

May the noble-minded scholars instead of cherishing ill-feeling kindly correct whatever errors have been committed through the dullness of my intellect in the way of wrong interpretations and misstatements.
Hemacandra
The author, Richard Osborne, was going to be a professional footballer. Instead he became a senior lecturer at London Guildhall University and is currently a freelance writer and teacher. He has lectured in Sydney and London and is the author of "The Radical Philosophy Reader" and of "Introducing Sociology".
The illustrator, Borin Van Loon, has toiled long into the night on "Introducing Buddha... Darwin... Genetics... Cultural Studies... Sociology... Mathematics..." (not necessarily in the same volume) and has written and illustrated books on dogs, DNA, domes and dreamlike comix.

Bibliography

Getting into Eastern Philosophy is not an easy task, partly because of the overlap between religion and philosophy that we discussed earlier. There are, however, some recent works that attempt to provide an overview.

This very recent interest is a product of the last ten years. Going back to the Classics themselves is always a good start, but they are often difficult to understand without any prior knowledge.

General Reading

These texts are all generally accessible to the non-philosopher and cover historical background as well as the philosophy.

Eberhard, W., **Conquerors and Rulers**. Leiden: E.J.Brill 1952
Hackett, S.C., **Oriental Philosophy: A Westerner's Guide to Eastern Thought**. Madison: University of Wisconsin Press 1979
Hinnells, J.R., **A Handbook of Living Religions**. London: Penguin 1984
Hope, J. & Van Loon, B., **Buddha for Beginners**. Cambridge: Icon Books 1994
Legge, J., **The Chinese Classics Vol.1**. Hong Kong: 1861.
Sastri, P.D., **The Essentials of Eastern Philosophy**. 1928 (Difficult to get hold of — should be reprinted.)
Schwartz, B., **The World of Thought in Ancient China**. Cambridge, Mass: Harvard University Press 1985
Sen, K.M., **Hinduism**. London: Penguin 1991
Smart, N., **The World's Religions**. Cambridge University Press 1989
Solomon, R.C. & Higgins, K.M., **World Philosophy — a Text with Readings**. McGraw-Hill 1995 (Short introduction to many world philosophies with readings.)
Cooper, D.E., **World Philosophies**. Blackwell 1995 (Wide overview at more difficult level.)

More Difficult General Texts

Basham, A.L., **The Wonder that was India**. London: Fontana 1971
Bonevac, D. & Phillips, S., **Understanding Non-Western Philosophy: Introductory Readings**. California: Mayfield Publishing 1993
Brannigan, M.C., **The Pulse of Wisdom**. Wadsworth Publishing 1995 (Quite dense overview with readings.)
Koller, J.M., **Oriental Philosophies**. New York: Charles Scribner & Sons 1985
Radhakrishnan, S., **Eastern Religions and Western Thought**. Oxford University Press 1992
Riepe, D. (ed), **Asian Philosophy Today**. New York: Gordon & Breach 1981

Hinduism
Brown, B., **The Wisdom of the Hindus**. New York: Garden City Publishing 1938
Hume, R.E., **The Thirteen Principal Upanishads** (2nd edn). Oxford University Press 1983
Isherwood, C. (ed), **Vedanta for the Western World**. London: Unwin Books 1963
Koller, J.M., **The Indian Way**. New York: Macmillan 1982
Moore, C., **The Indian Mind: Essentials of Indian Philosophy and Culture**. University of Hawaii Press 1967
Radhakrishnan, S., **Indian Philosophy** (2 vols). London: Allen & Unwin 1923
Raju, P.T., **The Philosophical Traditions of India**. London: Allen & Unwin 1971
Renou, L., **Religions of Ancient India**. New York: Schocken 1968
Smart, N., **Doctrine and Argument in Indian Philosophy**. London: Allen & Unwin 1964
Zaehner, R.C., **Hindu Scriptures**. London: Everyman's Library, J.M. Dent & Sons 1966
Weber, M., **The Religions of India**. Glencoe, Illinois: 1958

Chinese Philosophy
Allinson, R.E., **Understanding the Chinese Mind**. Hong Kong: Oxford University Press 1989
Bloom, I., **Knowledge Painfully Acquired: The K'un-chih chi by Lo Ch'in-shun**. New York: Columbia University Press 1987
Bodde, D., **Chinese Thought, Society and Science**. University of Hawaii Press 1991
Fung Yu-Lan, **A Short History of Chinese Philosophy**. New York: Free Press 1966 (The most concise and authoritative overview around.)
A History of Chinese Philosophy (2 vols). New Jersey: Princeton University Press 1952
Fung Yu-Lan, **The Spirit of Chinese Philosophy**. London: Routledge, Kegan & Paul 1962
Ch'eng, Chung Ying, **New Dimensions of Confucian and Neo-Confucian Philosophy**. Albany: State University of New York Press 1991
Confucius, **The Analects, The Great Learning and the Doctrine of the Mean**. New York: Dover Publications Inc. 1971
Creel, H.G., **Confucianism and the Chinese Way**. New York: 1960
Chang, Chung-yuan, **Creativity and Taoism**. New York: Harper & Row 1963
Cleary, T., **The Essential Tao**. San Francisco: Harper 1991
The I Ching or Book of Changes. New Jersey: Princeton University Press 1967
Sun Tzu, **The Art of War**. Oxford University Press 1963
Waley, A., **Three Ways of Thought in Ancient China**. London: Allen & Unwin 1939

Index

Advaita-Vedanta school 68–73
anatman 84
Aryans 28–9
asramas 39
atman 52
  as Brahman 44, 60, 73
avatar 54

Bhagavad-gita 53–5, 69
Bodhidharma 142
Book of Changes see I Ching
Brahma 44
Brahma-Sutra 69
Brahman 35, 69–73
Brahmans as priests 30
Buddhism 13, 21, 78–87
  China 138–44
  Japan 145–51

caste system 29–31
cause and effect 65
Chang Tsai 154–6
characteristics of Eastern philosophy 8
ch'i 154–60
China
  ancient dynasties 98
  Buddhism 138–44
  four phases 99
  and India 6–9
  modern 164–9
Chinese
  culture 92
  language 91
  philosophy 90–144
Chu-Tzu *see* School of Laws
Confucianism 110–22, 152–63
  those against 122
  main principles 112
Confucius 94, 106–9

darshana 56
Dewey, John 165
dharma 49, 53
  Buddhism 79–80
Dogen 150

East vs. West 11–17
Empirical school 163
Enlightenment 14, 21
eroticism 48
ethics 39

Four Noble Truths 80

God 15, 74–5
  Vaiseshika school 60
  see also Brahman; Krishna; T'ai Chi; Vishnu
Great Appendix to the Yi 137

Hegel, G.W.F. 17
Hindu schools 56
Hinduism 22–77
history 11
humanism 101

I Ching 100, 104
India and China 6–9
Indian philosophy 18–38
  seven phases 24–5
interconnectedness 16

Jainism 76–7
Japan, Buddhism 145–51
Japanese philosophy 9, 149

karma 16, 51
  Buddhism 85, 143
  and caste system 29–30
Kamasutra, the 48
Krishna 53–4

Lacan, Jacques 83
language 119
  see also under Chinese
Legalist school 124–5
li 157, 160
Liu Hsin 102–3

Madhva 74, 75
Mahabharata 53
Mahavira, Vardhamana 76
Maoism 167–70
Marxism *see* Maoism
maya 71
meditation 67, 150
Mencius 115–17
Mohist school 121–3
moksha 43, 50
monism 68

nirvana 50, 144
non-dualism 74
Nyaya school 57–9

On Contradiction 168

philosophy 3
  Japanese 9, 149
politics, neo-Confucian 161
postmodernity 171–2

Ramanuja 74
reality 8, 35, 36–7, 44
  Ramanuja 74
reincarnation 28, 38
  Buddhism 84
Russell, Bertrand 165

Samkhya school 62–5
samsara 10, 50, 52
Sankara 69
sannyasa 43
School
  of Laws 158–61
  of Mind 162–3
  of Names 118–20
self, the 34, 37
  and Buddhism 83
  defining 8
sex 47–8
Siddhartha *see* Buddhism
Six Classics, the 109
Spencer, Herbert 166
Sutra period 56–73

T'ai Chi 158
Tao
  book of 17
  school 126–37
time, nature of 151
Treasury of the True Dharma Eye 150
truth 14
  see also reality

universe, the 136
Upanishads 35–55, 69

Vaiseshika school 60–1
Vedanta *see Upanishads*
Vedas, the 21, 22, 28, 33
  and Buddhism 82
Vishnu 75

women 45–7

yeh *see* karma
Yen-Fu 166
Yin-Yang school 104–5
Yoga school 66–7

Zen Buddhism 145–51